Catching Life
by the Throat

Also by Josephine Hart

Damage
Sin
Oblivion
The Stillest Day
The Reconstructionist

Catching Life by the Throat

HOW TO READ POETRY AND WHY

Poems from Eight Great Poets

Josephine Hart

W. W. Norton & Company
New York • London

This compilation and introductory material Copyright © 2006 by Josephine Hart
First American Edition 2008

Complimentary CD, recording copyright (p) British Library Performances, in running
order, by: Ralph Fiennes, Juliet Stevenson, Edward Fox, Ian McDiarmid,
Helen McCrory, Roger Moore, Harold Pinter, Elizabeth McGoven, Harriet Walter,
Bob Geldof and Sinead Cusack

Photograph credits: W.H. Auden © Getty Images, Emily Dickinson © Getty Images,
T.S. Eliot © National Portrait Gallery, London, Rudyard Kipling © Roger Viollet/Getty
Images, Philip Larkin © estate of Fay Godwin/National Portrait Gallery, London,
Marianne Moore © Getty Images, Sylvia Plath © Corbis, William Butler Yeats ©
National Portrait Gallery, London

For information about special discounts for bulk purchases, please contact
W. W. Norton Special Sales at specialsales@wwnorton.com or 800-233-4830

Manufacturing by Courier Westford
Production manager: Anna Oler

Library of Congress Cataloging-in-Publication Data
Catching life by the throat : poems from eight great poets / [edited by] Josephine Hart.
— 1st American ed.
p. cm.
Includes bibliographical references and index.
ISBN 978-0-393-06607-4
1. English poetry—19th century. 2. English poetry—20th century. 3. American poetry—
19th century. 4. American poetry—20th century. 5. English poetry—19th century—
History and criticism. 6. English poetry—20th century—History and criticism.
7. American poetry—19th century—History and criticism. 8. American poetry—
20th century—History and criticism. I. Hart, Josephine.
PR1221.C34 2008
821'.808—dc22   2007 51986

W. W. Norton & Company, Inc.
500 Fifth Avenue, New York, N.Y. 10110
www.wwnorton.com

W. W. Norton & Company Ltd.
Castle House, 75/76 Wells Street, London W1T 3QT

1 2 3 4 5 6 7 8 9 0

This book is dedicated to the Art of the Actor
and to
the Poets who have shaped my life

CONTENTS

Catching Life
by the Throat

ACKNOWLEDGEMENTS

The acknowledgement of one's debt to others is, alas, no guarantee of repayment. My expression of deep gratitude to everyone involved in the creation of this book – and the accompanying CD – is sincere. It is also wholly inadequate.

I owe a supreme debt to: Dame Eileen Atkins, Claire Bloom, Simon Callow, Alan Cox, Brian Cox, Marton Csokas, Sinéad Cusack, Hugh Dancy, Joanna David, Ralph Fiennes, Peter Florence, Edward Fox, Bob Geldof, Alexander Gilmour, Julian Glover, Lord Gowrie (Grey), Rupert Graves, Robert Hardy, Tom Hollander, Jeremy Irons, Damian Lewis, Helen McCrory, Ian McDiarmid, Elizabeth McGovern, Sir Roger Moore, Sir John Mortimer, Harold Pinter, Edna O'Brien, Charlotte Rampling, Kelly Reilly, Juliet Stevenson, Mark Strong, Harriet Walter and Dominic West, without whose generosity and commitment there would have been no Poetry Hour; Lennie Goodings, my publisher at Virago Press, whose knowledge and professionalism was matched only by her dedication. Her team were invariably helpful; David Young, Chairman and Chief Executive of Hachette Book Group USA, for his immediate heartening response to the concept; Hachette Audio, and Sarah Shrubb whose organisation of the CD was a model of smooth efficiency; Ed Victor, as ever, 'the good shepherd' whose determined faith never faltered; Grainne Fox of Ed Victor Ltd, for her unstinting support and discerning advice; Angharad Wood of Tavistock Wood, whose insight and calm effectiveness were invaluable; Charles Finch who, with Harvey Nichols, launched our second season at a splendid lunch; Barbara Rafaeli and Bloomberg for their generous video recording of the events; Sir Peter Stothard, Peter Florence (who suggested the library as a venue) and Geordie Greig have been for years wise friends and supporters; the biographers and essayists on whose learning I have been so reliant and who are named, with deep admiration, in the source notes; Rose Astor, Emma Maher, J.S. Rafaeli, whose patient assistance has been much appreciated. Finally, my very special gratitude to The British Library – our home since January 2004. Lord Eatwell, Jill Finney, Lara Jukes, Heather Norman-Soderlind, the curators, Ken Shirreffs, Deborah Warner, Savan Modha have, since our first event, been consistently enthusiastic and totally efficient. They, with Virago Press and Hachette Audio have made possible the distribution of this book, the accompanying CD and a three-hour 3 CD audiobook free of charge to secondary schools. It is truly an astonishing act of generosity.

My family, Maurice, Adam and Edward loyally attended every poetry evening, and informed me that I was never less than brilliant. On such loving lies is a family built.

14 August 2006

INTRODUCTION

It has been a long love affair. It started with a *coup de foudre* in a house of God.

The setting was dramatic: a strange white cathedral, which, with *Fitzcarraldo*-like incongruity, stood ghostly sentinel against the grey skyline of an Irish Midlands town. 'In the beginning was the Word and the Word was with God and the Word was God' was probably the first line of pure poetry I ever heard. It remains, albeit to my now atheist's ear, perfect.

I was a word child, in a country of word children, where life was language before it was anything else. History made English the language that we lived. Though the many sins committed by its original practitioners were mournfully recited at my convent school the truth was clear to us all. English was the elite subject. It was taught with passion. I quickly learned, however, that my native country practised a literary hierarchical system of Orwellian precision: novels good, plays better, poetry best. Were not the signatories of the Irish Proclamation of Independence poets? Poets were not only heroes. they were indeed the gods of language.

At twelve every girl in my class could recite at least one Shakespeare sonnet, a minimum of four Yeats poems, some Eliot and Auden – carefully selected – and a number of poems by Gerard Manley Hopkins, Patrick Pearse, Alfred Tennyson and William Wordsworth – 'the holy time is quiet as a nun/breathless with adoration' had particular resonance. Even the tone deaf could hear the music of language. Our inner ear was being cultivated. When, at thirteen, we left for other schools, me to board, our pre-adolescent minds were already enchanted by Yeatsian dream imagery, challenged, if a little confused, by complex Eliot word-patterns and compelled by the religious lyricism of Hopkins. The harder poems were ahead of us but we were ready for them. Soon Eliot's mysterious 'footfalls' echoed 'in the memory'. Yeats, we discovered, deserted the fairy woods and moved into the darker territory of obsessive love; we learned that 'one man loved the pilgrim soul in you' – a serious lesson concerning erotic love. Browning's line, 'all smiles stopped together', stopped us in our tracks. Keats and Shelley taught us that we knew nothing. Frost, Lowell and Byron joined all the word warriors, arming us for life. Later Larkin loped in, Heaney and Hughes changed the landscape and Plath disturbed a universe.

What of novels and plays? The thrilling universe of characters and tales of incident and coincidence in great novels traced, for my adolescent soul, the strange arc of life. I read obsessively, both what was allowed and what was not. I can no longer remember which was which. I do remember the shocking worldliness of Balzac, the polite cruelty of Henry James, the sophisticated gender-games of Iris Murdoch, long before I fully understood their implications. Like many young girls I considered myself a actress. I read the plays it was not possible for me to see: Beckett, Pinter, Ionesco. I once tried to persuade the Mullingar Players to stage Ionesco's *The Chairs*. I failed. Eventually, many years later, I became a West End theatre producer, my instinct less than commercial. Lorca's *The House of Bernarda Alba*, Iris Murdoch's *The Black Prince*, Noël Coward's only tragedy *The Vortex*, were successful, but they were not, alas, the basis of a career, though they gave me a privileged view (from the wings) of the mysterious alchemy of theatre. Only Pirandello's *Six Characters in Search of an Author* captures quite how surreal the experience is.

However, I found in the key moments of my own life that the subtlety of character or plot which makes for great art in the novel or the theatre slipped away; the specific impact faded over time. Shakespeare I thought the only exception. Yet what I recalled from his plays were often fragments of speeches, rarely who spoke them or why. Poetry on the other hand, once it had seeped into my mind, surfaced at times of need, often becoming a lifeline. Poetry, this trinity of sound, sense and sensibility, gave voice to experience in a way no other literary art form could. It has never let me down. At various times it has provided me with a key to understanding; it has expressed what I believed inexpressible, whether of joy or despair; it provided me, a girl with no sense of direction, with a route map through life. It threw sudden shafts of light on my own soul and drew at least the shadow outline of the souls of others. It is the most, I now realise, that we are ever permitted to glimpse. Without poetry I would have found life less comprehensible, less bearable and infinitely less enjoyable.

What of poets on poetry? Poetry is 'one person talking to another' according to Eliot; 'The supreme fiction' for Wallace Stevens; 'If it makes my whole body so cold no fire can ever warm me, I know it's poetry' declared Emily Dickinson; 'A way of taking Life by the throat' for Robert Frost. This last inspired the title for this book, *Catching Life by the Throat*, and the accompanying CD. In the late 1980s, when I realised it was almost impossible to hear the work of the great, dead poets anywhere in London, I created Gallery Poets; an antidote, perhaps, to the absolute power of what Chesterton called 'the arrogant oligarchy who merely happen to be walking around'. I approached many of Britain's leading actors and with more passion than finesse asked them whether they would read the work of what I'd begun to see as my dead poets society. They all said yes. Actors still do, for no fee, for no expenses. Their generosity astonishes me. I decided to present the poetry in the context of the life of the poet and each evening began, as it still does, with a short introduction. 'A poet always writes out of his personal life; in his finest work out of its tragedy, whatever it may be, remorse, lost love, or loneliness' – Yeats. Even Eliot, that most private of poets, also believed that we understand the work better when we understand something of the poet's life.

Eventually, one of our most successful Gallery Poets productions – an Eliot evening, 'Let us go then, you and I', starring Eileen Atkins, Edward Fox and Michael Gough – transferred to the Lyric, Hammersmith, and from there to the Lyric in Shaftesbury Avenue, to cries of, 'Are you mad, Josephine?' It was, and is, the first and only time an evening of pure poetry had a West End run, helped no doubt by Valerie Grove's kind review: 'They queued and fought for tickets.'

In January 2004 we moved to the British Library and in their inti-
mate, 255-seat theatre we continue to present our monthly poetry
readings. Ticket costs are kept low – £5 or £7.50 – and all monies over
and above the costs of the British Library go to the Actors Centre.
The evenings are recorded and, with the help of the actors, the
publishers and the library. I am giving a copy of this book with its
accompanying CD, along with the full length three-hour CD, to
every secondary school (over 5,000) in the UK.

Why these particular poets? Why these particular poems? (It
proved just as difficult to choose eight poems by the less than prolific
Larkin, as eight from the thousand or so poems by Dickinson.) A
good poet, Eliot wrote, must not only have 'something to say, a little
different from what anyone has said before', he must also have found
the different way of saying it which expresses the difference in what
he is saying'. It's a demanding challenge. These poets meet it. The
poems – even the lighter ones – prove why. Each poet in many, if not
all, of these poems, also succeeds in the almost mystical weaving of
words that connects us to 'the auditory imagination'. This, Eliot's
insight of genius into the nature of the poetic gift, is 'the feeling for
syllable and rhythm, penetrating far below the conscious levels of
thought and feeling, invigorating every word; sinking to the most
primitive and forgotten, returning to an origin and bringing some-
thing back, fusing the most ancient and most civilised mentalities'. It
is *the* profound and rare poetic gift.

Many books provide an essential guide to the more technical
aspects of poetry – though this, alas, is not one of them. I draw some
comfort from Eliot's statement: 'I have never been able to retain the
names of feet and metre . . . if I wanted to know why one line was
good and another bad . . . scansion could not tell me.' Great lines are
those whose words 'have often a network of tentacular roots reaching
down to the deepest terrors and desires'. Thus, strangely, we recognise
the sound often before we comprehend the meaning.

The sense of sound and what Robert Frost described as 'the sound
of sense' is lost unless we *hear* it. The loss is incalculable. Increasingly
our inner ear is failing and an entire sound archive, from which great

poetry was not only created but appreciated and understood, is fading away. For centuries this inner ear was trained through the speaking of poetry aloud, the oral tradition not a discipline but a voluptuous joy as we absorbed into memory the resonance of sound. It is a privilege of which many, particularly children, are now deprived. 'Poetry,' Harold Bloom writes, 'helps us to speak to ourselves more clearly and more fully and to *overhear* that speaking.' Robert Frost's mantra, 'Writing with your ear to the voice', holds equally true for reading. All communication is transformed by sensitivity to the ebb and flow of sound within a sentence – 'language, caught alive'. Catching 'language alive' is a serious business.

Seamus Heaney, as an undergraduate at Queens University, Belfast, heard Eliot's *Four Quartets* spoken by the actor Robert Speaight. In his essay 'Learning from Eliot', he recalls how 'what I heard made sense'. Previously he'd been held at bay by the 'bigness of the structure', its 'opacity of thought'. On listening, however, he found that 'what was hypnotic read aloud had been perplexing when sight-read for meaning only.' Yeats, when he was seventy-two, claimed that he had spent his life 'clearing out of poetry every phrase written for the eye, and bringing all back to syntax, that is for ear alone'. From Auden, as ever, an absolute: 'No poem, which when mastered, is not better heard than read is good poetry.'

Hence our CD. W. H. Auden is read by Ralph Fiennes, T. S. Eliot by Edward Fox, Ian McDiarmid and Helen McCrory, Emily Dickinson by Juliet Stevenson, Rudyard Kipling by Roger Moore, Philip Larkin by Harold Pinter, Marianne Moore by Elizabeth McGovern, Sylvia Plath by Harriet Walter and W. B. Yeats by Sinéad Cusack and Bob Geldof – great voices speaking great lines. They not only love the poetry itself; they have, by instinct and training, an understanding of tone, rhythm and phrasing as they 'sound out' each poem. In that sounding out it's possible to enter the kingdom of poetry. And after that it's up to you.

W. H. AUDEN

Wystan Hugh Auden was born in York in 1907. A poet,
playwright, librettist and critic, his 1930 collection *Poems*
brought him instant fame. Awarded the Gold Medal for
Poetry in 1937 and the Pulitzer Prize in 1948, he was
Professor of Poetry at Oxford University from 1956 to
1961. He died in 1973.

W. H. AUDEN

Truth Out of Time

'One Sunday afternoon in March 1922, a school friend casually asked me if I wrote poetry. I, who had never written a line or even read one with pleasure, decided at that moment that poetry was my vocation.' Just like that. And therein lies the mystery of Auden. The critic and novelist John Bayley writes: 'That he turned out to be a brilliant poet . . . does not alter the arbitrariness of his decision to become one.' Art and will conjoined; fame and success followed. *Poems*, published in 1930 by Faber and Faber (T. S. Eliot's initial rejection had been a great disappointment), made his name and almost immediately. Edward Mendelson in his introduction to *The Collected Poems* points out that, in the history of English literature, only Byron became famous more quickly. Two further collections, *The Orators* (1932) and *Look Stranger!*, led to two Gold Medals for Poetry, one from the Queen, one from the King – George VI. During a lifetime as a poet, playwright, essayist and librettist, W. H. Auden garnered further awards and honours on both sides of the Atlantic. In America he won the Gold Medal for Poetry, the National Book Award and the Pulitzer Prize. In 1956 he was elected Professor of Poetry at Oxford University.

'Poetry', he once wrote, is 'memorable speech'. His poems contain some of the most succinct, elegant and unforgettable lines in literature. His psychological and philosophical insights into the workings of time, the nature of love, of isolation, the ethical choices of the state and the individual, sear themselves into our consciousness. A

9

poetic inquisitor, he drills deep in 'the deserts of the heart'. His poems throw down a moral challenge – can we win 'Truth out of Time'? Even in the gladiatorial arena of love and sex, an arena in human life in which self-deception often rules, he remains clear-sighted. His love for Chester Kallman, 'the wrong blond' (so named because Auden, who was expecting another male guest when Chester turned up at his hotel room, exclaimed, 'But it's the wrong blond!'), lasted on its own terms, mostly Chester's, for the rest of his life. 'The triple situation of being sexually jealous like a wife, anxious like a nanny, and competitive like a brother, is not easy for my kind of temperament. Still, it is my bed and I must lie on it.' He knew the cost when he wrote 'If equal affection cannot be/Let the more loving one be me'.

Auden, like Kipling, had a purpose. 'In so far as poetry, or any of the arts, can be said to have an ulterior purpose, it is, by telling the truth, to disenchant, and disintoxicate.' And yet he himself as Edward Mendelson points out had been 'enchanted'. One night in 1933, 'something happened': his 'Vision of Agape', captured in a Dali-like image, in the poem 'Out on the lawn I lie in bed'. Of this seminal experience Auden wrote, 'I felt myself invaded by a power which, though I consented to it, was irresistible and certainly not mine. For the first time in my life I knew exactly – because, thanks to the power, I was doing it – what it means to love one's neighbour as oneself.'

The disenchanter as an ecstatic points less to fierce internal conflict than to what John Bayley describes in his essay 'The Flight of the Enchanter' as a 'dualism' in Auden. Bayley notes that a certain vulnerability in the poet is cited in both Humphrey Carpenter's biography and Edward Mendelson's critical study as the possible cause. Charles Osborne in his biography notes the same lifelong trait. Evidently a favourite quotation of Auden's was that of Montaigne: 'We are, I know not how, double in ourselves, so that what we believe, we disbelieve and cannot rid ourselves of what we condemn.' Certainly it is impossible to miss the almost carefully balanced contradictions.

Born in York, in 1907, the youngest of three sons of a middle-class professional family, Wystan Hugh Auden became an Anglo-Catholic Communist and volunteered to fight in Spain in the civil war. Many believe he left the battlefield when England was itself at war (in fact, he left with Christopher Isherwood, in January 1939, before war was declared, volunteered in America and was turned down). He was a hugely disorganised man, one of the most sartorially challenged in literature, often wearing his socks on his head – yet his working hours were monastically disciplined. A homosexual, he married Thomas Mann's daughter Erika, who had been declared an enemy of the Nazi state. Marriage to Auden provided her with a passport. Christopher Isherwood, who had been initially approached, had rejected the idea. Honourably, Auden stepped in. 'Delighted,' he said. He may have believed that his dominant faculties were 'intellect and intuition', his weak ones 'feeling and sensation', yet he wrote one of the loveliest lyrics in the language: 'Lay your sleeping head, my love,/Human on my faithless arm;' An independent man, he nevertheless, even in his forties, feared loneliness. 'I shall,' he wrote, 'probably die alone at midnight, in a hotel, to the great annoyance of the management.' He did just that. In the Altenburgerhof, in Vienna, on 28 September 1973, Auden died of a heart attack, which he'd once told Charles Osborne was 'the nicest way' to go; 'it's cheap and it's quick.' He was definitely alone. The reaction of the management is not recorded.

The poetry of such a man should confuse. In fact, it has powerful simplicity. It is his pursuit of truth that gives his poetry its moral tone. His poems sound a warning bell. As they summon us to undo 'the folded lie,/The romantic lie in the brain/Of the sensual man-in-the-street' they also remind us: 'We must love one another or die.'

The Poems

'When I find myself in the company of scientists, I feel like a shabby curate who has strayed by mistake into a drawing room full of dukes.' Not the hierarchical position most poets award themselves. However, in these eight poems, Auden, the man who'd initially read Natural Sciences at university (before switching to English) and whose father was a doctor, uses language forensically and to the same purpose as the scientist: the revelation of truth. This pursuit is not necessarily driven by a Keatsian belief that 'Beauty is truth, truth beauty', rather more by conviction that we must bear witness to what is real. Heaney describes his poetry as 'magnificently sane'.

In 'Musée des Beaux Arts', the ship in Breughel's painting *Icarus* witnessed the fall, 'the white legs disappearing into the green/Water;', yet 'sailed calmly on'. 'The dreadful martyrdom must run its course' while we are 'eating or opening a window or just walking dully along'. Perhaps down Bristol Street, with the clocks chiming out 'You cannot conquer Time' as they do in 'As I Walked Out One Evening'. The poet reminds us 'In headaches and in worry/Vaguely life leaks away,/And Time will have his fancy/To-morrow or to-day.' Less *carpe diem* than acceptance that 'Life remains a blessing/Although you cannot bless.' And, even tougher, 'You shall love your crooked neighbour/With your crooked heart.' Philip Larkin noted the genius that allowed Auden to convey 'the inimitable Thirties fear, the sense that something was going to fall like rain' and, he added, 'The poetry is in the blaming and warning.' In 'September 1, 1939' the warning couldn't be clearer: 'I and the public know/What all schoolchildren learn,/Those to whom evil is done/Do evil in return.'

In 'Song of the Devil' contempt for man's ego and vanity drips from every mocking phrase. The three following poems are gentler but never soft. It's not his style. Of 'O Tell Me the Truth About Love',

Auden said, 'For me, personally, it was a very important poem. It's amazing how prophetic these things can be, because it was just after that that I met the person who did really change things for me completely.' (Enter Chester Kallman, bearing the gifts of beauty and, as a gifted librettist, brilliance.) in 'The Love Feast', Saint Augustine's cry of 'Give me chastity . . . but not yet' echoes in 'an upper room at midnight' as the narrator spots 'Miss Number in the corner/Playing hard to get.'

Auden writes, 'If I Could Tell You', but he doesn't. He can't. The reason? Love . . . In the poem 'In Memory of W. B. Yeats', Auden writes of his fellow poet whom 'Mad Ireland hurt . . . into poetry', and who 'disappeared in the dead of winter: . . . What instruments we have agree/The day of his death was a dark cold day.' Another line from the poem is equally appropriate to Auden. His 'gift survived it all.'

Musée des Beaux Arts

About suffering they were never wrong,
The Old Masters: how well they understood
Its human position; how it takes place
While someone else is eating or opening a window or just walking
    dully along;
How, when the aged are reverently, passionately waiting
For the miraculous birth, there always must be
Children who did not specially want it to happen, skating
On a pond at the edge of the wood:
They never forgot
That even the dreadful martyrdom must run its course
Anyhow in a corner, some untidy spot
Where the dogs go on with their doggy life and the torturer's horse
Scratches its innocent behind on a tree.

In Breughel's *Icarus*, for instance: how everything turns away
Quite leisurely from the disaster; the ploughman may
Have heard the splash, the forsaken cry,
But for him it was not an important failure; the sun shone
As it had to on the white legs disappearing into the green
Water; and the expensive delicate ship that must have seen
Something amazing, a boy falling out of the sky,
Had somewhere to get to and sailed calmly on.

As I Walked Out One Evening

As I walked out one evening,
 Walking down Bristol Street,
The crowds upon the pavement
 Were fields of harvest wheat.

And down by the brimming river
 I heard a lover sing
Under an arch of the railway:
 'Love has no ending.

'I'll love you, dear, I'll love you
 Till China and Africa meet,
And the river jumps over the mountain
 And the salmon sing in the street,

'I'll love you till the ocean
 Is folded and hung up to dry
And the seven stars go squawking
 Like geese about the sky.

'The years shall run like rabbits,
 For in my arms I hold
The Flower of the Ages,
 And the first love of the world.'

But all the clocks in the city
 Began to whirr and chime:
'O let not Time deceive you,
 You cannot conquer Time.

'In the burrows of the Nightmare
  Where Justice naked is,
Time watches from the shadow
  And coughs when you would kiss.

'In headaches and in worry
  Vaguely life leaks away,
And Time will have his fancy
  To-morrow or to-day.

'Into many a green valley
  Drifts the appalling snow;
Time breaks the threaded dances
  And the diver's brilliant bow.

'O plunge your hands in water,
  Plunge them in up to the wrist;
Stare, stare in the basin
  And wonder what you've missed.

'The glacier knocks in the cupboard,
  The desert sighs in the bed,
And the crack in the tea-cup opens
  A lane to the land of the dead.

'Where the beggars raffle the banknotes
  And the Giant is enchanting to Jack,
And the Lily-white Boy is a Roarer,
  And Jill goes down on her back.

'O look, look in the mirror,
  O look in your distress;
Life remains a blessing
  Although you cannot bless.

'O stand, stand at the window
   As the tears scald and start;
You shall love your crooked neighbour
   With your crooked heart.'

It was late, late in the evening,
   The lovers they were gone;
The clocks had ceased their chiming,
   And the deep river ran on.

September 1, 1939

I sit in one of the dives
On Fifty-Second Street
Uncertain and afraid
As the clever hopes expire
Of a low dishonest decade:
Waves of anger and fear
Circulate over the bright
And darkened lands of the earth,
Obsessing our private lives;
The unmentionable odour of death
Offends the September night.

Accurate scholarship can
Unearth the whole offence
From Luther until now
That has driven a culture mad,
Find what occurred at Linz,
What huge imago made
A psychopathic god:
I and the public know
What all schoolchildren learn,
Those to whom evil is done
Do evil in return.

Exiled Thucydides knew
All that a speech can say
About Democracy,
And what dictators do,

The elderly rubbish they talk
To an apathetic grave;
Analysed all in his book,
The enlightenment driven away,
The habit-forming pain,
Mismanagement and grief:
We must suffer them all again.

Into this neutral air
Where blind skyscrapers use
Their full height to proclaim
The strength of Collective Man,
Each language pours its vain
Competitive excuse:
But who can live for long
In an euphoric dream;
Out of the mirror they stare,
Imperialism's face
And the international wrong.

Faces along the bar
Cling to their average day:
The lights must never go out,
The music must always play,
All the conventions conspire
To make this fort assume
The furniture of home;
Lest we should see where we are,
Lost in a haunted wood,
Children afraid of the night
Who have never been happy or good.

The windiest militant trash
Important Persons shout
Is not so crude as our wish:

What mad Nijinsky wrote
About Diaghilev
Is true of the normal heart;
For the error bred in the bone
Of each woman and each man
Craves what it cannot have,
Not universal love
But to be loved alone.

From the conservative dark
Into the ethical life
The dense commuters come,
Repeating their morning vow,
'I *will* be true to the wife,
I'll concentrate more on my work',
And helpless governors wake
To resume their compulsory game:
Who can release them now,
Who can reach the deaf,
Who can speak for the dumb?

All I have is a voice
To undo the folded lie,
The romantic lie in the brain
Of the sensual man-in-the-street
And the lie of Authority
Whose buildings grope the sky:
There is no such thing as the State
And no one exists alone;
Hunger allows no choice
To the citizen or the police;
We must love one another or die.

Defenceless under the night
Our world in stupor lies;

Yet, dotted everywhere,
Ironic points of light
Flash out wherever the Just
Exchange their messages:
May I, composed like them
Of Eros and of dust,
Beleaguered by the same
Negation and despair,
Show an affirming flame.

Song of the Devil

(From 'Two Songs')

Ever since observation taught me temptation
Is a matter of timing, I've tried
To clothe my fiction in up-to-date diction,
The contemporary jargon of Pride.
    I can recall when, to win the more
        Obstinate round,
      The best bet was to say to them: 'Sin the more
        That Grace may abound.'

Since Social Psychology replaced Theology
The process goes twice as quick,
If a conscience is tender and loth to surrender
I have only to whisper: 'You're sick!
    Puritanical morality
        Is madly Non-U:
    Enhance your personality
        With a Romance, with two.

'If you pass up a dame, you've yourself to blame,
For shame is neurotic, so snatch!
All rules are too formal, in fact they're abnormal,
For any desire is natch.
    So take your proper share, man, of
        Dope and drink:
    Aren't you the Chairman of
        Ego, Inc.?

'Free-Will is a mystical myth as statistical
Methods have objectively shown,
A fad of the Churches: since the latest researches
Into Motivation it's known
    That Honor is hypocrisy,
        Honesty a joke.
    You live in a Democracy:
        Lie like other folk.

'Since men are like goods, what are shouldn'ts or shoulds
When you are the Leading Brand?
Let them all drop dead, you're way ahead,
Beat them up if they dare to demand
    What may your intention be,
        Or what might ensue:
    There's a difference of dimension be-
        -tween the rest and you.

'If in the scrimmage of business your image
Should ever tarnish or stale,
Public Relations can take it and make it
Shine like a Knight of the Grail.
    You can mark up the price that you sell at, if
        Your package has glamour and show:
    Values are relative.
        Dough is dough.

'So let each while you may think you're more O.K.,
More yourself than anyone else,
Till you find that you're hooked, your goose is cooked,
And you're only a cipher of Hell's.
    Believe while you can that I'm proud of you,
        Enjoy your dream:
    I'm so bored with the whole fucking crowd of you
        I could *scream*!'

O Tell Me the Truth About Love

(From 'Twelve Songs')

XII
Some say that love's a little boy,
 And some say it's a bird,
Some say it makes the world go round,
 And some say that's absurd,
And when I asked the man next-door,
 Who looked as if he knew,
His wife got very cross indeed,
 And said it wouldn't do.

Does it look like a pair of pyjamas,
 Or the ham in a temperance hotel?
Does its odour remind one of llamas,
 Or has it a comforting smell?
Is it prickly to touch as a hedge is,
 Or soft as eiderdown fluff?
Is it sharp or quite smooth at the edges?
 O tell me the truth about love.

Our history books refer to it
 In cryptic little notes,
It's quite a common topic on
 The Transatlantic boats;
I've found the subject mentioned in
 Accounts of suicides,
And even seen it scribbled on
 The backs of railway-guides.

Does it howl like a hungry Alsatian,
    Or boom like a military band?
Could one give a first-rate imitation
    On a saw or a Steinway Grand?
Is its singing at parties a riot?
    Does it only like Classical stuff?
Will it stop when one wants to be quiet?
    O tell me the truth about love.

I looked inside the summer-house;
    It wasn't ever there:
I tried the Thames at Maidenhead,
    And Brighton's bracing air.
I don't know what the blackbird sang,
    Or what the tulip said;
But it wasn't in the chicken-run,
    Or underneath the bed.

Can it pull extraordinary faces?
    Is it usually sick on a swing?
Does it spend all its time at the races,
    Or fiddling with pieces of string?
Has it views of its own about money?
    Does it think Patriotism enough?
Are its stories vulgar but funny?
    O tell me the truth about love.

When it comes, will it come without warning
    Just as I'm picking my nose?
Will it knock on my door in the morning,
    Or tread in the bus on my toes?
Will it come like a change in the weather?
    Will its greeting be courteous or rough?
Will it alter my life altogether?
    O tell me the truth about love.

The Love Feast

In an upper room at midnight
See us gathered on behalf
Of love according to the gospel
Of the radio-phonograph.

Lou is telling Anne what Molly
Said to Mark behind her back;
Jack likes Jill who worships George
Who has the hots for Jack.

Catechumens make their entrance;
Steep enthusiastic eyes
Flicker after tits and baskets;
Someone vomits; someone cries.

Willy cannot bear his father,
Lilian is afraid of kids;
The Love that rules the sun and stars
Permits what He forbids.

Adrian's pleasure-loving dachshund
In a sinner's lap lies curled;
Drunken absent-minded fingers
Pat a sinless world.

Who is Jenny lying to
In her call, Collect, to Rome?
The Love that made her out of nothing
Tells me to go home.

But that Miss Number in the corner
Playing hard to get . . .
I am sorry I'm not sorry . . .
Make me chaste, Lord, but not yet.

If I Could Tell You

Time will say nothing but I told you so,
Time only knows the price we have to pay;
If I could tell you I would let you know.

If we should weep when clowns put on their show,
If we should stumble when musicians play,
Time will say nothing but I told you so.

There are no fortunes to be told, although,
Because I love you more than I can say,
If I could tell you I would let you know.

The winds must come from somewhere when they blow,
There must be reasons why the leaves decay;
Time will say nothing but I told you so.

Perhaps the roses really want to grow,
The vision seriously intends to stay;
If I could tell you I would let you know.

Suppose the lions all get up and go,
And all the brooks and soldiers run away;
Will Time say nothing but I told you so?
If I could tell you I would let you know.

In Memory of W. B. Yeats

(d. January 1939)

I

He disappeared in the dead of winter:
The brooks were frozen, the airports almost deserted,
And snow disfigured the public statues;
The mercury sank in the mouth of the dying day.
What instruments we have agree
The day of his death was a dark cold day.

Far from his illness
The wolves ran on through the evergreen forests,
The peasant river was untempted by the fashionable quays;
By mourning tongues
The death of the poet was kept from his poems.

But for him it was his last afternoon as himself,
An afternoon of nurses and rumours;
The provinces of his body revolted,
The squares of his mind were empty,
Silence invaded the suburbs,
The current of his feeling failed: he became his admirers.

Now he is scattered among a hundred cities
And wholly given over to unfamiliar affections,
To find his happiness in another kind of wood
And be punished under a foreign code of conscience.
The words of a dead man
Are modified in the guts of the living.

But in the importance and noise of to-morrow
When the brokers are roaring like beasts on the floor of the Bourse,
And the poor have the sufferings to which they are fairly
    accustomed,
And each in the cell of himself is almost convinced of his freedom,
A few thousand will think of this day
As one thinks of a day when one did something slightly unusual.
What instruments we have agree
The day of his death was a dark cold day.

II
You were silly like us: your gift survived it all:
The parish of rich women, physical decay,
Yourself. Mad Ireland hurt you into poetry.
Now Ireland has her madness and her weather still,
For poetry makes nothing happen: it survives
In the valley of its saying where executives
Would never want to tamper, flows on south
From ranches of isolation and the busy griefs,
Raw towns that we believe and die in; it survives,
A way of happening, a mouth.

III
Earth, receive an honoured guest:
William Yeats is laid to rest.
Let the Irish vessel lie
Emptied of its poetry.

In the nightmare of the dark
All the dogs of Europe bark,
And the living nations wait,
Each sequestered in its hate;

Intellectual disgrace
Stares from every human face,

And the seas of pity lie
Locked and frozen in each eye.

Follow, poet, follow right
To the bottom of the night,
With your unconstraining voice
Still persuade us to rejoice;

With the farming of a verse
Make a vineyard of the curse,
Sing of human unsuccess
In a rapture of distress;

In the deserts of the heart
Let the healing fountain start,
In the prison of his days
Teach the free man how to praise.

EMILY DICKINSON

Born in Amherst, Massachusetts in 1830, Emily Elizabeth
Dickinson, unpublished in her lifetime, has long been
recognised as one of America's great nineteenth-century
poets. She died in 1886.

EMILY DICKINSON

Heavenly Hurt

When she died in 1886 at the age of fifty-six, Emily Dickinson, the New England spinster daughter of Emily Norcross Dickinson and Edward Dickinson, prominent lawyer and one-time representative to Congress, whose heart, she said, was 'pure and terrible such as I have found in no other', did not have a single book of poetry to her name. Days after her death, her sister Lavinia opened her bureau, in the room that Emily always kept locked, and found, neatly copied and sewn together in groups, over nine hundred poems. The number would eventually total 1,775. Emily Dickinson's is the most remarkable story in the history of literature. Eventually, after four years of bitter family disputes, which became known as the Emily Dickinson wars, her first book of poetry was published and became the literary event of 1890. However, it was not until 1955, when the family's oddly touching, artistically disastrous, editorial 'tidying up' process was reversed (they had removed the dashes, dots and capitals that were crucial to her poetic code), that the sheer elemental ferocity of Emily Dickinson's poetry was released.

'Publication – is the Auction/Of the Mind' may be the opening lines of one of her poems, as is 'Fame is a fickle food.' However, during her lifetime she had secretly tried for both, and failed. She tried again and failed again – she knew why 'Success is counted sweetest/By those who ne'er succeed'. On 15 April 1862 – a date that Thomas H. Johnson describes in his introduction to *The Complete Poems* as one of the most significant in American nineteenth-century literature – Emily Dickinson sent four poems to Thomas Wentworth

Higginson. She had written to Higginson in response to an article of his for *Atlantic Monthly*. His 'Letter to a Young Contributor' – advice to those who wished to be published – included the admonition, 'Charge your style with life.' Higginson was unaware, as Johnson points out, that Emily Dickinson, then thirty-one, had already written over three hundred poems.

The four he received were shocking enough. Johnson quotes Higginson speaking years later of their impact. 'The impression of a wholly new and original poetic genius was as distinct on my mind at the first reading of these four poems as it is now, after thirty years of further knowledge; and with it came the problem never yet solved, what place ought to be assigned in literature to what is so remarkable, yet so elusive of criticism.' He declined to publish the poems as he thought them 'extreme'. They were: extreme works of genius. 'Strangeness' is, Harold Bloom writes, 'one of the prime requirements for entrance into the Canon'. Emily Dickinson certainly qualified. Bloom declared her 'as individual a thinker as Dante'. She sent three more poems to Higginson. Again, he was confounded. Below is the famous letter that she sent on 7 June 1862 to Higginson, it having taken her less than two months to signal her retreat from the public arena. Note its construction, the dashes, the dots, the capitals.

> I smile when you suggest that I delay "to publish" – that being foreign to my thought, as Firmament to Fin.
>
> If fame belonged to me, I could not escape her – if she did not, the longest day would pass me on the chase – and the approbation of my Dog, would forsake me – then. My Barefoot-Rank is better.
>
> You think my gait "spasmodic." I am in danger, Sir.
>
> You think me "uncontrolled." I have no Tribunal.' . . .
>
> The Sailor cannot see the North, but knows the Needle can.

It is one of the most elegant exits in literary history. Though she was to continue a correspondence with Higginson, there were to be no more efforts at publication. She withdrew to her genius and lived quietly with it for the rest of her life. 'I don't go from home, unless emergency take me by the hand.' Ecstatics often withdraw. The intensity with which they react to experience often makes its curtailment necessary. St Teresa of Avila – who was 'in the world but not of it' as my mother constantly reminded me: a maternal warning against worldliness – withdrew to a convent. The poet and ecstatic Gerard Manley Hopkins – whose piety was such that in gardens he walked with his head bowed, in order not to be distracted from the worship of God by the beauty of roses (a favourite tale of the nuns) – found solace in a monastery. Emily Dickinson simply stayed at home. Unlike novelist Jane Austen, who in an equally small world looked out at her '3 or 4 families' and created a universe, Dickinson looked inward, and in what Ted Hughes called her 'tranced suspense' came closer than any other writer to the depiction of the sublime. He quotes her reaction to the visit of a circus: 'Friday I tasted life. It was a vast morsel. A Circus passed the house – still I feel the red in my mind.' For such a temperament, her elective, virtual imprisonment in her house was either an act of psychological wisdom or one which made 'the smallest event an immensity' as Ted Hughes believed.

Reclusive, however, is not the same as shy. Emily Dickinson was very popular at school, and later proved an excellent hostess in her father's house (her prizewinning bread was often served). Ted Hughes points out that when in 1870 she finally met the key literary figure in her life, Thomas Wentworth Higginson, he seemed stunned by the 'very wantonness of overstatement' in the conversation of 'his half-cracked poetess', adding: 'I was never with anyone who drained my nerve power so much.' Her description of herself, prior to their meeting, speaks of a considerable self-confidence in her appearance and most especially her colouring. The 'nun of Amherst', as she was eventually called, was not veiled, though she remained hidden. 'I am small like the Wren, and my hair is bold, like the Chestnut bur – and my eyes, like the Sherry in the Glass, that the Guest leaves.' Read it again. Imagine it without the capitals and note that the guest has already drunk his sherry but has left enough in the glass to reflect the colour of her eyes. It is a compelling image, all the more so when one realises that Emily Dickinson suffered from a serious and extremely painful eye condition, possibly rheumatic iritis according to biographer Connie Ann Kirk, who stresses that the poet may have feared the loss of her sight (she shares this awful terror with Joyce and Milton who finally became wholly blind). Emily Dickinson's poetic 'vision' therefore becomes ever more complex; her line, 'Renunciation – is a piercing Virtue', for example, now reads differently. Judith Farr in her introduction to a collection of critical essays makes the intriguing point that, in Emily Dickinson's poetry, wordplay on 'I' and 'eye' occurs in literally hundreds of poems. Whether in her poetry or prose, behind the originality and the glittering brilliance lies something mysterious, shadow-light behind the closed door.

Emily Dickinson is sometimes thought of as a great religious poet. However, she obeyed her own rules, not necessarily those of the Church, which she often refused to visit. Her God was her own. Ted Hughes, whose insight has particular weight in the light of his own marriage to an ecstatic and a poet, Sylvia Plath, notes that 'vision, and the crowded, beloved Creation around her and Death – became her Holy Trinity.' Such passion in real life might well have overwhelmed the object of its affection. Was there an object of affection, of desire? If there was, his identity remains obscure. Harold Bloom says of her work, 'It is a drama of erotic loss.' What is certain is that between 1858 and 1862, she wrote the so-called 'master letters', which continue to puzzle scholars. They are passionate, intimate, full of longing. They were also probably never sent. In what are known as 'the flood years', 1860–66, Emily Dickinson wrote over a thousand poems. They range from 'Given in Marriage unto Thee', and 'Rearrange a "Wife's" affection', passionate poems, full of longing, which give way to poems of loss, such as 'Heart! We will forget him!', shame even, 'Not with a Club, the Heart is broken' resignation, 'After great pain, a formal feeling comes' and the oft-quoted 'My life closed twice'. Perhaps in Hughes' haunting phrase Emily Dickinson realised that her 'unusual endowment of love was not going to be asked for'.

The Poems

Emily Dickinson wrote short. Short does not mean sweet. Short does not mean easy. Just in case you think you can wing it with the nun of Amherst, let me quote Harold Bloom: 'One's mind had better be at its rare best' when reading Dickinson. Approach her with humility and full attention – she has a mind like a laser beam and she can seriously damage your complacency. 'My Life had stood – a Loaded Gun'. So does the poetry. She was an aristocrat of the soul and 'The Soul selects her own Society' is less spiritual hauteur than moral dignity. She also had great strength of character. It is, as Shelley noted, extraordinarily difficult to continue writing with no hope of publication. Her poem 'Success is counted sweetest/By those who ne'er succeed' may in its opening lines speak of that ironic wisdom. However, what follows are not three short verses bewailing her lack of recognition. What we hear is the same 'distant strains of triumph' that the defeated, dying soldier hears and the pain of his cruelly untimely death is 'agonized and clear'. The note, nevertheless, is not political. The poem was written in 1859; the Civil War did not begin until 1861. Though the threat of war and war itself were a constant, and her own poetry is often fiercely violent, Emily Dickinson was possibly the least political poet in nineteenth-century literature. It is perverse wisdom perhaps.

Death, and not only in war, is so close in Dickinson – her elective and constant companion of the imagination that every sense is sickle-sharpened, most particularly the sense of sound in 'I heard a Fly buzz'. As in the three following poems the note is one of great stillness, indeed of resignation. They disconcert with strange, cryptic power. 'A certain Slant of Light/. . . oppresses, like the Heft/Of Cathedral Tunes/When it comes . . ./Shadows – hold their breath'. Impossible, almost, not to hold one's own. 'Because I could not stop for Death –

/He kindly stopped for me—' is a shocking and unforgettable opening. 'After great pain, a formal feeling comes' (the selection of the word 'formal' is a mark of great emotional insight) and 'My life closed twice before its close–' bring death and the maiden ever closer. The 'death' in the last poem freezes us in the icy waters of lost love – a parting no less terrible than the second, indeed, almost secondary, final death. Philip Larkin, whose own obsession with death was as extreme as that of Dickinson, found her poetry 'odd', which in itself is odd. 'Poetry,' he said, is 'an affair of sanity' and he went on to list the 'big sane boys Chaucer, Shakespeare, Wordsworth and Hardy . . . the object of writing is to show life as it is, and if you don't see it like that you're in trouble, not life.' We're all in trouble, as he well knew, and that's the trouble with life. This unlikely juxtaposition of Dickinson and Larkin proves only John Bayley's point that 'Poetry wanders through the mysterious implications of its own exactness.' Exactly.

My Life had stood — a Loaded Gun —

My Life had stood – a Loaded Gun –
In Corners – till a Day
The Owner passed – identified –
And carried Me away –

And now We roam in Sovereign Woods –
And now We hunt the Doe –
And every time I speak for Him –
The Mountains straight reply –

And do I smile, such cordial light
Upon the Valley glow –
It is as a Vesuvian face
Had let its pleasure through –

And when at Night – Our good Day done –
I guard My Master's Head –
'Tis better than the Eider-Duck's
Deep Pillow – to have shared –

To foe of His – I'm deadly foe –
None stir the second time –
On whom I lay a Yellow Eye –
Or an emphatic Thumb –

Though I than He – may longer live
He longer must – than I –
For I have but the power to kill,
Without – the power to die –

The Soul selects her own Society —

The Soul selects her own Society –
Then – shuts the Door –
To her divine Majority –
Present no more –

Unmoved – she notes the Chariots – pausing –
At her low Gate –
Unmoved – an Emperor be kneeling
Upon her Mat –

I've known her – from an ample nation –
Choose One –
Then – close the Valves of her attention –
Like Stone –

Success is counted sweetest

Success is counted sweetest
By those who ne'er succeed.
To comprehend a nectar
Requires sorest need.

Not one of all the purple Host
Who took the Flag today
Can tell the definition
So clear of Victory

As he defeated – dying –
On whose forbidden ear
The distant strains of triumph
Burst agonized and clear!

I heard a Fly buzz — when I died —

I heard a Fly buzz – when I died –
The Stillness in the Room
Was like the Stillness in the Air –
Between the Heaves of Storm –

The Eyes around – had wrung them dry –
And Breaths were gathering firm
For that last Onset – when the King
Be witnessed – in the Room –

I willed my Keepsakes – Signed away
What portion of me be
Assignable – and then it was
There interposed a Fly –

With Blue – uncertain stumbling Buzz –
Between the light – and me –
And then the Windows failed – and then
I could not see to see –

There's a certain Slant of Light

There's a certain Slant of Light,
Winter Afternoons –
That oppresses, like the Heft
Of Cathedral Tunes –

Heavenly Hurt, it gives us –
We can find no scar,
But internal difference,
Where the Meanings, are –

None may teach it – Any –
'Tis the Seal Despair –
An imperial affliction
Sent us of the Air –

When it comes, the Landscape listens –
Shadows – hold their breath –
When it goes, 'tis like the Distance
On the look of Death –

Because I could not stop for Death —

Because I could not stop for Death –
He kindly stopped for me –
The Carriage held but just Ourselves –
And Immortality.

We slowly drove – He knew no haste
And I had put away
My labor and my leisure too,
For His Civility –

We passed the School, where Children strove
At Recess – in the Ring –
We passed the Fields of Gazing Grain –
We passed the Setting Sun –

Or rather – He passed Us –
The Dews drew quivering and chill –
For only Gossamer, my Gown –
My Tippet – only Tulle –

We paused before a House that seemed
A Swelling of the Ground –
The Roof was scarcely visible –
The Cornice – in the Ground –

Since then – 'tis Centuries – and yet
Feels shorter than the Day
I first surmised the Horses' Heads
Were toward Eternity –

After great pain, a formal feeling comes —

After great pain, a formal feeling comes –
The Nerves sit ceremonious, like Tombs –
The stiff Heart questions was it He, that bore,
And Yesterday, or Centuries before?

The Feet, mechanical, go round –
Of Ground, or Air, or Ought –
A Wooden way
Regardless grown,
A Quartz contentment, like a stone –

This is the Hour of Lead –
Remembered, if outlived,
As Freezing persons, recollect the Snow –
First – Chill – then Stupor – then the letting go –

My life closed twice before its close —

My life closed twice before its close —
It yet remains to see
If Immortality unveil
A third event to me

So huge, so hopeless to conceive
As these that twice befell.
Parting is all we know of heaven,
And all we need of hell.

T. S. ELIOT

Thomas Stearns Eliot, born in St Louis, Missouri in 1888, was a poet, playwright and critic. His *Prufrock and Observations*, *The Waste Land* and *Four Quartets* are masterpieces of the twentieth century. He won the Nobel Prize in 1948 and died in 1965.

T. S. ELIOT

I Gotta Use Words When I Talk to You

Virginia Woolf to T. S. Eliot: 'We're not as good as Keats.' T. S. Eliot to Virginia Woolf: 'Oh yes, we are. We're trying something harder.' Checkmate! It's a delightful vignette, one of many, in Peter Ackroyd's brilliant biography. T. S. Eliot was indeed trying something harder and he succeeded. With the publication of *The Waste Land*, Eliot broke the mould in poetry, in the same way that Joyce's *Ulysses* – published the same year, 1922 – broke the mould in the novel. In the history of poetry there is before and after Thomas Stearns Eliot.

Who was he, this man who created a new movement in literature, virtually a new poetic language that has 'the capacity to cut into our consciousness with the sharpness of a diamond' (Anders Österling, Permanent Secretary to The Swedish Academy 1948)? What was he like, this man about whom Ted Hughes said, 'There is a direct line which can be traced from Virgil to Dante, from Dante to Milton and from Milton to Eliot, the greatest poet for over three hundred years'?

Well, the greatest poet for over three hundred years was described by John Betjeman as 'a quiet, remote figure'. At Lloyd's Bank, where he worked as a clerk, he cut a figure of great elegance but he was in fact very good at his job. After the bank years, he became editor, and then director, at publishers Faber and Gwyer (later Faber and Faber), where he was known as 'the Pope of Russell Square'. Even after he'd begun to make a name for himself as a poet, Ackroyd notes that Eliot did not exactly dazzle those who met him. The society hostess Lady Ottoline Morrell found him 'dull, dull, dull'. Aldous Huxley said Eliot

51

was 'just another Europeanised American talking about French literature in the most uninspiring fashion'. 'The dull, dull man', 'the boring Europeanised American', who even described himself, in less than thrilling terms, as 'Classical in literature, Royalist in politics and Anglo-Catholic in religion', was born in St Louis, Missouri, in September 1888, a late son to older parents who already had four daughters and a son. They were, Ackroyd writes, successful, practical Unitarians, part of the intellectual aristocracy of America. 'They never did less than was expected of them and Eliot too did what was expected of him.' He went to the right schools, the right clubs and the right university, Harvard, where, in the library one day, he came across Arthur Symons' *The Symbolist Movement in Literature*. Its main practitioners were French – Mallarmé, Verlaine, Rimbaud and Laforgue. The discovery of this book was, Eliot himself said, life-changing. The importance he attached from then on to the *symbol* of reality, and its associations and affinities, is key to 'experiencing' Eliot. Mood, subtle connections, strange conjunctions, in language and image – rather than realism of time and place and incident – all work together in an Eliot poem with almost hypnotic power. This Eliot effect I noted again and again at readings, even during his most demanding work. The hour-long *Four Quartets*, for example, is listened to in a concentrated silence even during long, often daunting passages.

After Harvard his path was deemed to be clear: academe. He rebelled and left for Paris in the autumn of 1910. It would not be his last determined departure and from Harvard to Paris is not only a question of geography. Through his friendship with a fellow lodger, Jean Verdenal, Eliot quickly became part of the heady literary life of Paris. By 1911, Eliot was scribbling in a notebook the poem that Ezra Pound would call the first American masterpiece of the twentieth century, 'The Love Song of J. Alfred Prufrock' (later dedicated to Verdenal, who was killed in the war). He was also writing 'Portrait of a Lady'. He was just twenty-two and it is one of literature's more unnerving facts that he had already taken possession of his gift. The writer Conrad Aiken, Eliot's Harvard friend, is quoted by Ackroyd as having been astonished at 'how sharp and complete and sui generis the whole thing was from the outset . . . The *wholeness* is there, from the beginning.' One journey, from Harvard to Paris, had resulted in great intellectual and artistic riches. Another journey, from Paris to Oxford's Merton College, led him to a darker, personal destiny: marriage to Vivien Haigh-Wood. She it was who would shape his life and influence his work for decades to come. The artistic riches in future would be dearly bought.

Eliot was twenty-seven in 1915 when he met Vivien and, he said later, 'very young for his age, very timid, very inexperienced'. They married quickly, Eliot seemingly wholly unaware that Vivien suffered from a severe hormonal disorder. The morphine-based drugs that were used to treat her exacerbated her often hysterical, sometimes dangerous, behaviour. Over the years the huge financial burden of doctors and sanatoria meant that he rarely worked fewer than fifteen hours a day. The stress almost broke his health. If it was hard for Eliot, it destroyed Vivien. It is a terrible tale and biographers – Ackroyd, Lyndall Gordon and others – approach it with compassion. The American critic Cynthia Ozick is rather harsher in her judgement of Eliot's emotional and psychological journey, which she describes as one from compassion to horror. In 1933, after eighteen years of marriage, he left Vivien, ostensibly to give a series of lectures in Harvard. He had no intention of returning to her. She refused to accept the inevitable. Her illness and her distress led to behaviour that was regarded, in those more constrained times, as bordering on insanity. She was confined for the last years of her life to a mental institution, where she died in 1947. Eliot never visited during that time. *Four Quartets*, which he started in 1936, three years after their separation and published in its entirety in 1943, is his mature masterpiece and it led to his being awarded the Nobel Prize for literature in 1948. 'The more perfect the artist,' he once wrote, 'the more completely separate in him will be the man who suffers and the mind which creates.' Maybe. However, only a man who had suffered deeply could write that one of 'the gifts reserved for age' is 'the awareness of things ill done and done to others' harm/Which once you took for exercise of virtue'.

Late in life, he made a kind of dash for the adult happiness that had eluded him. He married Valerie Fletcher, his young assistant at Faber. It was a marriage that transformed him. This most private of poets wrote of his deep joy in 'A dedication to my Wife', a love poem of 'private words addressed to you in public'. He was now an iconic figure, fêted everywhere he went. 'Viva, Viva, Eliot,' they called to him in Rome and Ackroyd tells us he once gave a lecture to 14,000 people in a football stadium in Minnesota on 'The Frontiers of Criticism'. Those were the days! However, although there were plays and essays, there was to be no more poetry. Larkin's 'rare bird' had flown away.

Eliot died in 1965, aged seventy-seven, with his second wife Valerie at his side. After his death she said he felt he had paid too high a price for poetry. 'The dead writers are that which we know,' he once said. The Nobel academy agreed: 'Tradition is not a dead load which we drag along with us . . . it is the soil in which the seeds of coming harvests are to be sown, and from which future harvests will be garnered.'

The Waste Land

Where is it? What is it? It's a state of mind. It continues to induce in the reader what Cyril Connolly described as 'the almost drugged and haunted condition' that it induced in undergraduates in 1922 as they gathered together to read it aloud. Peter Ackroyd notes its 'echoic quality which requires the inflection of the voice of the reader to give it shape'. The writer Edmund Wilson called it 'the great knockout up to date'. It still is.

The original title was 'He Do the Police in Different Voices'. It's Betty Higden's phrase from Dickens' *Our Mutual Friend*: 'You mightn't think it, but Sloppy is a beautiful reader of a newspaper. He do the police in different voices.' Eliot 'do' *The Waste Land* in different voices, many different voices – a multiplicity of sound. Soloists, as in a choir, break in and out of the song. The lines of gender are often blurred. They tell of strange visions interposed with fragments of memory, sometimes in different languages, incorporating lines from Dante, Sanskrit texts or the Bible, occasionally using jazz rhythms (Larkin once noted that jazz is the closest to the unconscious that we have). At other times they sing raucous popular songs, followed by a sudden switch of tone to the formality of Elizabethan language or the incantations of a prayer. 'A Game of Chess' (the second movement) opens slowly in the room, which is heavy with 'her strange synthetic perfumes'. Then, suddenly, the jagged voice of the hysterical woman breaks in – 'My nerves are bad to-night. Yes, bad.' – and then 'What are you thinking of? What thinking? What?' The note is both frightening and sad – then it fades away into 'O O O O that Shakespeherian Rag—' after which, unexpectedly, we're transported to a cockney pub where the landlord recounts the tale of 'poor Albert' who has 'been in the army four years, he wants a good time', and 'Lil' who 'ought to be ashamed', 'because she looks 'so antique'. As closing time approaches he calls out, repeatedly, 'HURRY UP PLEASE ITS TIME' (the meaning of the line multi-layered) and he fades away with echoing, gentle salutation 'Good night, ladies, good night, sweet ladies, good night,/good night.' The incomparable soaring genius of the piece, with Eliot the composer and the conductor of its five movements, makes reading *The Waste Land* one of the most thrilling experiences in literature. And life.

What was Eliot's own state of mind when he wrote it and does it matter as one listens or reads the poems? The answer is no. But the question is interesting and has some bearing on the second section of *The Waste Land*, 'A Game of Chess'. This is acknowledged to be, in part, a portrait of his marriage to Vivien Haigh-Wood. In the margin of the dialogue of the nervous, harassed woman, Vivien wrote 'wonderful, wonderful'. A letter from Eliot to British novelist Sydney Schiff, dated November 1921, concerning Part Three of *The Waste Land*, may come as a surprise to those who underestimate Vivien's influence. 'I have done a rough draft but do not know whether it will do, and must wait for Vivien's opinion as to whether it is printable.' According to Ackroyd, Vivien once replied to a question concerning Eliot: 'Tom's mind? I am Tom's mind.' The reason for their estrangement, with its terrible consequence, did not lie in creative dissonance. This marriage, which he said later 'brought to her no happiness', brought to him 'the state of mind out of which came *The Waste Land*'. And that, to many, is a shocking admission from the man to whom the theory of 'impersonality' in art was crucial.

Yet, as John Bayley points out, 'The interior of Eliot's poetry is deeply personal, full of secrets and intimacies.' In his own notes to *The Waste Land*, Eliot quotes F. H. Bradley: 'My experience falls within my own circle, a circle closed on the outside.' How could it be otherwise? Within his own 'circle of experience' at that time lay long days at the bank and a home life that increasingly resembled that of a sanatorium. Vivien's suffering was extreme: 'Have you ever been in such incessant pain that you felt your sanity was going . . . that's the way she is,' he wrote in a letter in 1921. The 'outside' was post-war depression and exhaustion, as well as the slow grief of Europe and

Britain having seen a generation wiped out. The summer of 1921 was a summer of drought and severe influenza. Eliot, Ackroyd points out, was ill and exhausted and found it enormously difficult to write. He quotes Siegfried Sassoon as having heard Eliot declare around that time, 'All great art is based on a condition of fundamental boredom – passionate boredom.' It was Vivien who encouraged *him* to go to a sanatorium in Lausanne and here *The Waste Land* was born.

It was to have as editor one of the great literary midwives in the history of poetry – the amazing Ezra Pound. When he read it for the first time he wrote to Eliot, 'Complimenti, you bitch. I am wracked by the seven jealousies.' What poet wouldn't be? However, in the British Library, Eliot's original copy is marked through with so many red pencil lines that it resembles a piece of modern art. Ezra Pound, the ruthless surgeon and dedicated friend, cut to the music and carved away anything that dulled the note. *The Waste Land* is dedicated, as it should be, to Ezra Pound *il migliore fabbro* – the better craftsman.

'The Love Song of J. Alfred Prufrock'
'Portrait of a Lady'
'The Hollow Men'

'It is an art of the nerves, this art of Laforgue, and it is what all art would tend towards if we followed our nerves on all our journeys.' These lines come from Symons' *The Symbolist Movement in Literature* concerning the poet Jules Laforgue. 'Eliot followed his nerves in Prufrock' is C. K. Stead's brilliant insight in an essay full of brilliant insights. This journey of the nerves was to last a lifetime and at considerable cost to Eliot's health. Though 'The Love Song of J. Alfred Prufrock' is now acknowledged as the first great poem of the twentieth century, Eliot was 'heartlessly indifferent to its fate' according to Conrad Aiken, who, with Ezra Pound, tried everyone they could think of to have it published. It was no easy task as Ackroyd notes. One publisher turned it down on the basis that 'it's completely insane'.

Do not ask 'What is it?' Accept J. Alfred's invitation: 'Let us go then, you and I'. You will never regret accompanying the middle-aged narrator on his visit. C. K. Stead notes however, that Eliot, in a conversation with Hugh Kenner, disputed the term 'middle-aged': 'Prufrock is a young man.' Of whatever age, he is the repressed, inadequate 'attendant lord' whose surname once adorned a hardware shop in Eliot's home town of St Louis. When asked about 'the love life of J. Alfred Prufrock', Eliot replied, 'I'm afraid that J. Alfred Prufrock didn't have much of a love life.'

The lady in 'Portrait of a Lady' may have suffered a similar fate. It is another poem of nervous tension and the constant possibility of explosive anger. The hyper-awareness of the narrator – not only to the actual words but to the undernote in each statement of 'The Lady' – creates a mood of claustrophobic unease in this piece, often described as the shortest one-act play in literature. She was, according to Ackroyd, Miss Adelaide Moffatt whom Eliot used to visit to 'take tea' and he believes that she represented a Boston way of life with which Eliot was becoming increasingly frustrated. Many find amusement in this poem. I've always found it to be one of subtle, polite cruelty. The chasm between the two individuals is unbridgeable and not just because of the age differential. Their conversation is a duet of misunderstanding and misapprehension, and eventually sadness as she becomes increasingly aware that what she'd hoped for is slipping away into the colder actuality of their relationship. 'I have been wondering frequently of late/(But our beginnings never know our ends!)/Why we have not developed into friends.' The unnamed narrator ponders a final, more cruel question: '. . . what if she should die some afternoon . . ./And should I have the right to smile?' Ironic? Yes, brutally so.

'The Hollow Men' was influenced by Brutus' line from *Julius Caesar*, 'Between the acting of a dreadful thing/And the first motion, all the interim is/Like a phantasma, or a hideous dream:', which in Eliot becomes 'Between the idea/And the reality/Between the motion/And the act/Falls the Shadow'. The iconic line from Conrad's masterpiece *Heart of Darkness* 'Mistah Kurtz – he dead.' – is epigram to the poem. In Francis Coppola's film *Apocalypse Now* Marlon Brando speaks the lines: 'We are the hollow men/ We are the stuffed men/Leaning together/Headpiece filled with straw. Alas!' Heaney calls it, 'Rare music'. It certainly is – down to the last beat: *'This is the way the world ends/Not with a bang but a whimper.'*

The Love Song of J. Alfred Prufrock

S'io credessi che mia risposta fosse
A persona che mai tornasse al mondo,
Questa fiamma staria senza più scosse.
Ma per ciò che giammai di questo fondo
Non tornò viva alcun, s'i'odo il vero,
Senza tema d'infamia ti rispondo.

Let us go then, you and I,
When the evening is spread out against the sky
Like a patient etherised upon a table;
Let us go, through certain half-deserted streets,
The muttering retreats
Of restless nights in one-night cheap hotels
And sawdust restaurants with oyster-shells:
Streets that follow like a tedious argument
Of insidious intent
To lead you to an overwhelming question . . .
Oh, do not ask, 'What is it?'
Let us go and make our visit.

In the room the women come and go
Talking of Michelangelo.

The yellow fog that rubs its back upon the window-panes,
The yellow smoke that rubs its muzzle on the window-panes,
Licked its tongue into the corners of the evening,
Lingered upon the pools that stand in drains,
Let fall upon its back the soot that falls from chimneys,

Slipped by the terrace, made a sudden leap,
And seeing that it was a soft October night,
Curled once about the house, and fell asleep.

And indeed there will be time
For the yellow smoke that slides along the street
Rubbing its back upon the window-panes;
There will be time, there will be time
To prepare a face to meet the faces that you meet;
There will be time to murder and create,
And time for all the works and days of hands
That lift and drop a question on your plate;
Time for you and time for me,
And time yet for a hundred indecisions,
And for a hundred visions and revisions,
Before the taking of a toast and tea.

In the room the women come and go
Talking of Michelangelo.

And indeed there will be time
To wonder, 'Do I dare?' and, 'Do I dare?'
Time to turn back and descend the stair,
With a bald spot in the middle of my hair—
(They will say: 'How his hair is growing thin!')
My morning coat, my collar mounting firmly to the chin
My necktie rich and modest, but asserted by a simple pin—
(They will say: 'But how his arms and legs are thin!')
Do I dare
Disturb the universe?
In a minute there is time
For decisions and revisions which a minute will reverse.

For I have known them all already, known them all—
Have known the evenings, mornings, afternoons,

I have measured out my life with coffee spoons;
I know the voices dying with a dying fall
Beneath the music from a farther room.
    So how should I presume?

    And I have known the eyes already, known them all—
The eyes that fix you in a formulated phrase,
And when I am formulated, sprawling on a pin,
When I am pinned and wriggling on the wall,
Then how should I begin
To spit out all the butt-ends of my days and ways?
    And how should I presume?

    And I have known the arms already, known them all—
Arms that are braceleted and white and bare
(But in the lamplight, downed with light brown hair!)
Is it perfume from a dress
That makes me so digress?
Arms that lie along a table, or wrap about a shawl.
    And should I then presume?
    And how should I begin?

. . . . .

    Shall I say, I have gone at dusk through narrow streets
And watched the smoke that rises from the pipes
Of lonely men in shirt-sleeves, leaning out of windows? . . .

    I should have been a pair of ragged claws
Scuttling across the floors of silent seas.

. . . . .

    And the afternoon, the evening, sleeps so peacefully!
Smoothed by long fingers,

Asleep . . . tired . . . or it malingers,
Stretched on the floor, here beside you and me.
Should I, after tea and cakes and ices,
Have the strength to force the moment to its crisis?
But though I have wept and fasted, wept and prayed,
Though I have seen my head (grown slightly bald) brought in upon
    a platter,
I am no prophet – and here's no great matter;
I have seen the moment of my greatness flicker,
And I have seen the eternal Footman hold my coat, and snicker,
And in short, I was afraid.

    And would it have been worth it, after all,
After the cups, the marmalade, the tea,
Among the porcelain, among some talk of you and me,
Would it have been worth while,
To have bitten off the matter with a smile,
To have squeezed the universe into a ball
To roll it toward some overwhelming question,
To say: 'I am Lazarus, come from the dead,
Come back to tell you all, I shall tell you all'—
If one, settling a pillow by her head,
    Should say: 'That is not what I meant at all.
    That is not it, at all.'

    And would it have been worth it, after all,
Would it have been worth while,
After the sunsets and the dooryards and the sprinkled streets,
After the novels, after the teacups, after the skirts that trail along
    the floor—
And this, and so much more?—
It is impossible to say just what I mean!
But as if a magic lantern threw the nerves in patterns on a screen:
Would it have been worth while
If one, settling a pillow or throwing off a shawl,

And turning toward the window, should say:
   'That is not it at all,
   That is not what I meant, at all.'

     . . . . .

   'No! I am not Prince Hamlet, nor was meant to be;
Am an attendant lord, one that will do
To swell a progress, start a scene or two,
Advise the prince; no doubt, an easy tool,
Deferential, glad to be of use,
Politic, cautious, and meticulous;
Full of high sentence, but a bit obtuse;
At times, indeed, almost ridiculous –
Almost, at times, the Fool.

   I grow old . . . I grow old . . .
I shall wear the bottoms of my trousers rolled.

   Shall I part my hair behind? Do I dare to eat a peach?
I shall wear white flannel trousers, and walk upon the beach.
I have heard the mermaids singing, each to each.

I do not think that they will sing to me.

   I have seen them riding seaward on the waves
Combing the white hair of the waves blown back
When the wind blows the water white and black.

   We have lingered in the chambers of the sea
By sea-girls wreathed with seaweed red and brown
Till human voices wake us, and we drown.

Portrait of a Lady

Thou hast committed –
Fornication: but that was in another country,
And besides, the wench is dead.

The Jew of Malta

I

 Among the smoke and fog of a December afternoon
You have the scene arrange itself—as it will seem to do—
With 'I have saved this afternoon for you';
And four wax candles in the darkened room,
Four rings of light upon the ceiling overhead,
An atmosphere of Juliet's tomb
Prepared for all the things to be said, or left unsaid.
We have been, let us say, to hear the latest Pole
Transmit the Preludes, through his hair and finger-tips.
'So intimate, this Chopin, that I think his soul
Should be resurrected only among friends
Some two or three, who will not touch the bloom
That is rubbed and questioned in the concert room.'
—And so the conversation slips
Among velleities and carefully caught regrets
Through attenuated tones of violins
Mingled with remote cornets
And begins.
'You do not know how much they mean to me, my friends,
And how, how rare and strange it is, to find
In a life composed so much, so much of odds and ends,
(For indeed I do not love it . . . you knew? you are not blind!

How keen you are!)
To find a friend who has these qualities,
Who has, and gives
Those qualities upon which friendship lives.
How much it means that I say this to you—
Without these friendships—life, what *cauchemar!*'

　Among the windings of the violins
And the ariettes
Of cracked cornets
Inside my brain a dull tom-tom begins
Absurdly hammering a prelude of its own,
Capricious monotone
That is at least one definite 'false note'.
—Let us take the air, in a tobacco trance,
Admire the monuments,
Discuss the late events,
Correct our watches by the public clocks.
Then sit for half an hour and drink our bocks.

II
　Now that lilacs are in bloom
She has a bowl of lilacs in her room
And twists one in her fingers while she talks.
'Ah, my friend, you do not know, you do not know
What life is, you who hold it in your hands';
(Slowly twisting the lilac stalks)
'You let it flow from you, you let it flow,
And youth is cruel, and has no more remorse
And smiles at situations which it cannot see.'
I smile, of course,
And go on drinking tea.

　'Yet with these April sunsets, that somehow recall
My buried life, and Paris in the Spring,

I feel immeasurably at peace, and find the world
To be wonderful and youthful, after all.'

    The voice returns like the insistent out-of-tune
Of a broken violin on an August afternoon:
'I am always sure that you understand
My feelings, always sure that you feel,
  Sure that across the gulf you reach your hand.

    You are invulnerable, you have no Achilles' heel.
You will go on, and when you have prevailed
You can say: at this point many a one has failed.
But what have I, but what have I, my friend,
To give you, what can you receive from me?
Only the friendship and the sympathy
Of one about to reach her journey's end.

    I shall sit here, serving tea to friends . . .'

    I take my hat: how can I make a cowardly amends
For what she has said to me?
You will see me any morning in the park
Reading the comics and the sporting page.
Particularly I remark
An English countess goes upon the stage.
A Greek was murdered at a Polish dance,
Another bank defaulter has confessed.
I keep my countenance,
I remain self-possessed
Except when a street-piano, mechanical and tired
Reiterates some worn-out common song
With the smell of hyacinths across the garden
Recalling things that other people have desired.
Are these ideas right or wrong?

III

The October night comes down; returning as before
Except for a slight sensation of being ill at ease
I mount the stairs and turn the handle of the door
And feel as if I had mounted on my hands and knees.
'And so you are going abroad; and when do you return?
But that's a useless question.
You hardly know when you are coming back,
You will find so much to learn.'
My smile falls heavily among the bric-à-brac.

'Perhaps you can write to me.'
My self-possession flares up for a second;
This is as I had reckoned.
'I have been wondering frequently of late
(But our beginnings never know our ends!)
Why we have not developed into friends.'
I feel like one who smiles, and turning shall remark
Suddenly, his expression in a glass.
My self-possession gutters; we are really in the dark.

'For everybody said so, all our friends,
They all were sure our feelings would relate
So closely! I myself can hardly understand.
We must leave it now to fate.
You will write, at any rate.
Perhaps it is not too late.
I shall sit here, serving tea to friends.'

And I must borrow every changing shape
To find expression . . . dance, dance
Like a dancing bear,
Cry like a parrot, chatter like an ape.
Let us take the air, in a tobacco trance—

Well! and what if she should die some afternoon,
Afternoon grey and smoky, evening yellow and rose;
Should die and leave me sitting pen in hand
With the smoke coming down above the housetops;
Doubtful, for a while
Not knowing what to feel or if I understand
Or whether wise or foolish, tardy or too soon . . .
Would she not have the advantage, after all?
This music is successful with a 'dying fall'
Now that we talk of dying—
And should I have the right to smile?

The Hollow Men

[A penny for the Old Guy]

I

We are the hollow men
We are the stuffed men
Leaning together
Headpiece filled with straw. Alas!
Our dried voices, when
We whisper together
Are quiet and meaningless
As wind in dry grass
Or rats' feet over broken glass
In our dry cellar

Shape without form, shade without colour,
Paralysed force, gesture without motion;

Those who have crossed
With direct eyes, to death's other Kingdom
Remember us—if at all—not as lost
Violent souls, but only
As the hollow men
The stuffed men.

II

Eyes I dare not meet in dreams
In death's dream kingdom
These do not appear:
There, the eyes are

Sunlight on a broken column
There, is a tree swinging
And voices are
In the wind's singing
More distant and more solemn
Than a fading star.

Let me be no nearer
In death's dream kingdom
Let me also wear
Such deliberate disguises
Rat's coat, crowskin, crossed staves
In a field
Behaving as the wind behaves
No nearer—

Not that final meeting
In the twilight kingdom

III
This is the dead land
This is cactus land
Here the stone images
Are raised, here they receive
The supplication of a dead man's hand
Under the twinkle of a fading star.

Is it like this
In death's other kingdom
Waking alone
At the hour when we are
Trembling with tenderness
Lips that would kiss
Form prayers to broken stone.

IV

The eyes are not here
There are no eyes here
In this valley of dying stars
In this hollow valley
This broken jaw of our lost kingdoms

In this last of meeting places
We grope together
And avoid speech
Gathered on this beach of the tumid river

Sightless, unless
The eyes reappear
As the perpetual star
Multifoliate rose
Of death's twilight kingdom
The hope only
Of empty men.

V

Here we go round the prickly pear
Prickly pear prickly pear
Here we go round the prickly pear
At five o'clock in the morning.

Between the idea
And the reality
Between the motion
And the act
Falls the Shadow

For Thine is the Kingdom

Between the conception
And the creation

Between the emotion
And the response
Falls the Shadow

Life is very long

Between the desire
And the spasm
Between the potency
And the existence
Between the essence
And the descent
Falls the Shadow

For Thine is the Kingdom

For Thine is
Life is
For Thine is the

This is the way the world ends
This is the way the world ends
This is the way the world ends
Not with a bang but a whimper.

The Waste Land

II. A Game of Chess

The Chair she sat in, like a burnished throne,
Glowed on the marble, where the glass
Held up by standards wrought with fruited vines
From which a golden Cupidon peeped out
(Another hid his eyes behind his wing)
Doubled the flames of sevenbranched candelabra
Reflecting light upon the table as
The glitter of her jewels rose to meet it,
From satin cases poured in rich profusion.
In vials of ivory and coloured glass
Unstoppered, lurked her strange synthetic perfumes,
Unguent, powdered, or liquid – troubled, confused
And drowned the sense in odours; stirred by the air
That freshened from the window, these ascended
In fattening the prolonged candle-flames,
Flung their smoke into the laquearia,
Stirring the pattern on the coffered ceiling.
Huge sea-wood fed with copper
Burned green and orange, framed by the coloured stone,
In which sad light a carvèd dolphin swam.
Above the antique mantel was displayed
As though a window gave upon the sylvan scene
The change of Philomel, by the barbarous king
So rudely forced; yet there the nightingale
Filled all the desert with inviolable voice
And still she cried, and still the world pursues,
'Jug Jug' to dirty ears.

And other withered stumps of time
Were told upon the walls; staring forms
Leaned out, leaning, hushing the room enclosed.
Footsteps shuffled on the stair.
Under the firelight, under the brush, her hair
Spread out in fiery points
Glowed into words, then would be savagely still.

   'My nerves are bad to-night. Yes, bad, Stay with me.
Speak to me. Why do you never speak. Speak.
      What are you thinking of? What thinking? What?
I never know what you are thinking. Think.'

   I think we are in rats' alley
Where the dead men lost their bones.

   'What is that noise?'
              The wind under the door.
'What is that noise now? What is the wind doing?'
        Nothing again nothing.
                            'Do
'You know nothing? Do you see nothing? Do you remember
Nothing?'

   I remember
Those are pearls that were his eyes.
'Are you alive, or not? Is there nothing in your head?'

                          But
O O O O that Shakespeherian Rag —
It's so elegant
So intelligent
'What shall 1 do now? What shall 1 do?
I shall rush out as I am, and walk the street
With my hair down, so. What shall we do tomorrow?

What shall we ever do?'
         The hot water at ten.
And if it rains, a closed car at four.
And we shall play a game of chess,
Pressing lidless eyes and waiting for a knock upon the door.

    When Lil's husband got demobbed, I said—
I didn't mince my words, I said to her myself
HURRY UP PLEASE ITS TIME
Now Albert's coming back, make yourself a bit smart.
He'll want to know what you done with that money he gave you
To get yourself some teeth. He did, I was there.
You have them all out, Lil, and get a nice set,
He said, I swear, I can't bear to look at you.
And no more can't I, I said, and think of poor Albert,
He's been in the army four years, he wants a good time,
And if you don't give it him, there's others will, I said.
Oh is there, she said. Something o' that, I said.
Then I'll know who to thank, she said, and give me a straight look.
HURRY UP PLEASE ITS TIME
If you don't like it you can get on with it, I said.
Others can pick and choose if you can't.
But if Albert makes off, it won't be for lack of telling.
You ought to be ashamed, I said, to look so antique.
(And her only thirty-one.)
1 can't help it, she said, pulling a long face,
It's them pills I took, to bring it off, she said.
(She's had five already, and nearly died of young George.)
The chemist said it would be all right, but I've never been the same.
You *are* a proper fool, I said,
Well, if Albert won't leave you alone, there it is, I said,
What you get married for if you don't want children?
HURRY UP PLEASE ITS TIME
Well, that Sunday Albert was home, they had a hot gammon,
And they asked me in to dinner, to get the beauty of it hot—

HURRY UP PLEASE ITS TIME
HURRY UP PLEASE ITS TIME
Goonight Bill. Goonight Lou. Goonight May. Goonight.
Ta ta. Goonight. Goonight.
Good night, ladies, good night, sweet ladies, good night,
    good night.

RUDYARD KIPLING

Poet, novelist and short story writer, Rudyard Kipling was
born of English parents in Bombay in 1865. His
Departmental Ditties (1886) and *Barrack-Room Ballads*
(1892) brought him world-wide fame. He won the Nobel
Prize in 1907, the first Englishman to be so honoured. He
died in 1936.

RUDYARD KIPLING

Word Warrior

The English, he believed, were slow to hate. If they need a master-class, Kipling's their man. Seamus Heaney famously uses his pen 'to dig with'. Kipling used his as a lethal weapon. He was a word warrior and he was well armed. The day of judgement may indeed have been round the corner but Kipling couldn't wait that long. He took aim at what he saw as injustice and incompetence, dishonesty and disloyalty, vanity and villainy, targeting those responsible: criminally negligent generals, venal politicians, corrupt businessmen, brutal authority fig-ures – most particularly those cruel to children, fired and gravely wounded them. If, as Eliot said, Kipling 'is not only serious, he has a vocation', it was that of literary marksman.

Like all good soldiers he was also a lookout scout. He had an uncanny sense of when and where trouble was brewing and the warn-ing note was swiftly sounded. M. M. Kaye's introduction to the collected works quotes Mark Twain: 'Kipling is the only living person not head of state whose voice is heard around the world the moment it drops a remark. The only such voice in existence that does not go by slow ship and rail but always travels first-class by cable.' Americans, Kaye notes, revered Kipling and when, aged thirty-four, he almost died from pneumonia, 'in the street outside his hotel in New York bark was spread to lessen the noise of passing traffic'. Yet he had no official position politically, economically or militarily. He was a passionate child of Empire, a fact as central to his life as Jean-Paul Sartre's Communism was to his. He believed it quite simply to be a power for good. Unlike other passionate believers in a political world view (Msr. Sartre again springs to mind) Kipling exposed the fault lines in the system, ruthlessly.

Although 'The White Man's Burden' in a sense became Kipling's own, he was not a fascist. 'He was further away from being a fascist as the most humane or the most progressive person is able to be,' declared George Orwell, in his otherwise not uncritical essay on Kipling. Of 'Gehazi' (concerning the Marconi scandal of 1912), one of Kipling's most notorious poems, Ian Gilmour states 'that it is neither evil nor anti-semitic'. Kipling was undoubtedly capable of a Larkinesque mockery of national characteristics but he was democratic in his selection of his target. Few nations escaped, except, surprisingly, the French whom he seemed to love. He was always wholly unimpressed by rank, whether military or social. 'English literature has no adequate account of the British soldier, what he thought of the night before battle, what he thought of his officers, between Henry V and Rudyard Kipling': M. M. Kaye, again. Orwell agrees: 'He had far more interest in the common soldier and far more anxiety that he get a fair deal than most liberals.' Kipling also regularly expressed his contempt for 'the flannelled fools at the wickets or the muddied oafs at the goals'.

Rudyard Kipling was a poet whose collected works run to just under seven hundred pages; a novelist – Kim is his masterpiece; a short story writer – his later ones, which Edmund Wilson called 'The Kipling Whom Nobody Read', are sublime, as are the children's books, The Jungle Book and The Just So Stories. He was also a journalist and a pamphleteer. He was, said Henry James, 'the most complete man of genius I have ever met'. In addition, Kipling was the first Englishman to win a Nobel Prize for Literature and was also its youngest recipient. Something of Myself is the apt title of his autobiography because something is all you get. Eliot said of him, he is 'the most inscrutable of authors . . . a writer impossible wholly to understand and quite impossible to belittle'.

He was born in 1865 in Bombay. His father, John Lockwood Kipling, a 'serene and tolerant man' according to Kipling, taught at the school of art. His mother, née Alice MacDonald, was, he said, 'all Celt and three parts fire'. Andrew Lycett in his perceptive biography quotes a family member as saying: 'It was impossible to predict how she would react at any given point.' She was also a talented musician from whom Kipling said he inherited no musical talent whatever, except what he described as 'the brute instinct for the beat necessary for the manufacture of verse'. Rather romantically his mother and father named their first-born after Lake Rudyard in Staffordshire, where they had first met at a picnic. Up to the age of five Rudyard Kipling was, it would seem, thoroughly spoiled. If his tantrums were epic – M. M. Kaye tells us of the small boy who, on a visit to Sussex, stamps off to the village warning inhabitants to get out of the way as there was an angry Rudy coming – the cure was savage. The loving parents, in a stunning act of psychological cruelty, left him, aged five, with his sister Trix, aged three, in a boarding house in Bournemouth, the subject of the bitterly sad short story, 'Baa, Baa, Black Sheep'. From this 'House of Desolation' as he called it in his memoirs, he and Trix attended a local school. It was to be five years before they saw their mother again and seven years before they saw their father. If an unhappy childhood is a great gift to a writer, then Kipling was truly blessed.

Eventually he was rescued and sent to boarding school. Although he was hugely clever, on being told that there was no money for university he returned to India and became a journalist in Lahore. He lived happily with his parents, whom he never seemed to have wished to wound, and when Trix returned Kaye points out that he referred contentedly to them as the 'Family Square'. By the time he reached the age of twenty-three, his *Departmental Ditties* and *Plain Tales From the Hills* were sold at every railway station in India – where, incidentally, he actually lived for fewer than ten years of his adult life. With the publication of *Barrack-Room Ballads* in 1892, when he was twenty-seven, he became world famous.

All biographers refer to his genuine modesty. He regarded himself as a craftsman. He was not greedy for honours for himself, turning down a knighthood, the poet laureateship and the Order of Merit. Though he had little time for 'the long-haired literati', he refused to criticise any 'fellow craftsman's output'. He had respect for the work of others from sea captains to civil servants; C. S. Lewis called him 'the poet of work'. 'Writers', he said, 'must recognise the gulf that separates even the least of those who do things worthy of being written about from even the best of those who have written things worthy of being talked about.' Not a universal attitude.

Few writers have travelled so much or have lived on so many continents. He witnessed national wars, world war and 'the savage wars of peace'. He lived to see his beloved Empire all but disintegrate. In his own life he suffered the tragedy of the death of his children – his daughter Josephine, who died from pneumonia when aged six, and his only son John, who died in the war. Eliot once wrote of Yeats: 'He was capable of experience,' and pointed to the late poetic development that ensued. That does not seem to have happened with Kipling. Though as John Bayley points out he became wiser. His extraordinary diversity in form and in subject matter has at its core emotional, moral and philosophical consistency. There is also something else, an elemental force that is as disturbing as it is unforgettable. Eliot wrote of him, 'There is always something alien about Kipling, as of a visitor from another planet . . . Kipling knew something of things which are beyond the frontier . . . a queer gift of second-sight, of transmitting messages from elsewhere, a gift so disconcerting when we are made aware of it that henceforth we are never quite sure when it is *not* present.' Kipling on every level makes us uneasy, his ferocity often frightens us, his perverse naivety unnerves us, his imperialism embarrasses us, and yet he continues on, an Immortal. The poems in this book are just eight of the many reasons why . . .

The Poems

First to Kipling and the women, of whom, in his personal life, there were virtually none. He married his wife Carrie, Caroline Starr Ballestier, after an awkward courtship. He was, in fact, liberal in sexual matters and certainly no innocent. His short story, 'Mrs Bathurst', is one of the most sexually shocking in literature. He fought hard for better medical facilities for women in India and was bitterly opposed to the custom of child brides. 'The Female Of The Species' is a delightfully provocative poem that often leads to spirited debate between the sexes. The winner is not a surprise.

From one battlefield to another: fathers and sons. 'Never seen Death yet, Dickie? Well, now is your time to learn,' It's not a sentimental education! 'The "Mary Gloster"' is one of the great dramatic monologues. 'Sir Anthony Gloster, dying, a baronite:' places on the shoulders of his despised son, Dickie, a task equal, almost, to that of Hamlet – but kinder in its way.

To real wars and warnings of war. 'Recessional' was published in *The Times* in 1897 to mark Queen Victoria's sixty years on the throne. Its iconic line, 'Lest we forget-' is a not jingoistic celebration. The Queen's Trumpeter, as he is here (when he died he was referred to as 'The King's Trumpeter'), sounds a warning note. Though he was much pilloried for the line 'lesser breeds without the Law', which is often interpreted as 'natives', Kipling was in fact referring to the Germans, who were anything but powerless at the time. They became stronger, as they proved in 1914.

'The Gods of the Copybook Headings' was published in October 1919 and, as Andrew Lycett writes in his biography, 'not only was England drained – so was Kipling. He was fifty-three. His son John was dead.' The exhaustion is clear in the poem, which asks how often must we relearn the old lessons. 'Copybooks' (which lasted in Ireland much longer than in England) were, as Lycett describes them, 'little ruled exercise books used to practise one's handwriting by copying – slowly and carefully – usually twenty times the line of a prayer, proverb or quotation.'

To two war poems. Kipling did not regret the war. Jorge Luis Borges writes that Kipling 'saw war as an obligation, but he never sang of victory, only of the peace that victory brings, and of the hardships of battle'. Execution in war is not only reserved for the enemy. 'Danny Deever' is the poem, above all others, that made Kipling as famous in England as he was in India. Professor Mason, an expert on Milton, is said by Kaye to have excitedly waved a copy at his students and cried out, 'Here's Literature! Here's Literature, at last.' He was right. It's a masterpiece of poetic, rhythmic perfection. As Eliot notes, 'in the combination of heavy beat and variation of pace . . . in the regular recurrence of same end words' you can hear the marching feet and the 'movement of the men in disciplined formation'. In the end, it is the pity that lingers, 'after hangin' Danny Deever in the mornin''. 'Tommy' is the ordinary soldier thrown out of bars and theatres while on leave, 'But it's "Thin red line of 'eroes" when the drums begin to roll'. It's a poem to make you hang your head in shame. As Orwell wrote, 'A humanitarian is always a hypocrite' and he quoted the line, 'makin' mock o' uniforms that guard you while you sleep'.

'The Children' is dedicated to John Kipling, killed on his first day of active service at the battle of Loos, where '8,246 men out of 10,000 were killed or wounded in 200 minutes.' The title is interesting in using the plural. 'One can't let one's friends' and neighbours' sons be killed in order to save us and our son,' Carrie Kipling said to a neighbour. Many of the greatest anti-war lines were written by a man often regarded as a warmonger. In 'Epitaphs of the War' Kipling gives individual voice to 'Mine angry and defrauded young' who, like his son John, were mown down in their hundreds of thousands, wave after wave of them marching towards the guns. 'If any question why we died,/Tell them, because our fathers lied.' Nothing changes.

The Female Of The Species

When the Himalayan peasant meets the he-bear in his pride,
He shouts to scare the monster, who will often turn aside.
But the she-bear thus accosted rends the peasant tooth and nail.
For the female of the species is more deadly than the male.

When Nag the basking cobra hears the careless foot of man,
He will sometimes wriggle sideways and avoid it as he can.
But his mate makes no such motion where she camps beside the
    trail.
For the female of the species is more deadly than the male.

When the early Jesuit fathers preached to Hurons and Choctaws,
They prayed to be delivered from the vengeance of the squaws.
'Twas the women, not the warriors, turned those stark enthusiasts
    pale.
For the female of the species is more deadly than the male.

Man's timid heart is bursting with the things he must not say,
For the Woman that God gave him isn't his to give away;
But when hunter meets with husband, each confirms the other's
    tale—
The female of the species is more deadly than the male.

Man, a bear in most relations—worm and savage otherwise,—
Man propounds negotiations, Man accepts the compromise.
Very rarely will he squarely push the logic of a fact
To its ultimate conclusion in unmitigated act.

Fear, or foolishness, impels him, ere he lay the wicked low,
To concede some form of trial even to his fiercest foe.
Mirth obscene diverts his anger! Doubt and Pity oft perplex
Him in dealing with an issue—to the scandal of The Sex!

But the Woman that God gave him, every fibre of her frame
Proves her launched for one sole issue, armed and engined for the
    same;
And to serve that single issue, lest the generations fail,
The female of the species must be deadlier than the male.

She who faces Death by torture for each life beneath her breast
May not deal in doubt or pity—must not swerve for fact or jest.
These be purely male diversions—not in these her honour dwells.
She the Other Law we live by, is that Law and nothing else.

She can bring no more to living than the powers that make her
    great
As the Mother of the Infant and the Mistress of the Mate!
And when Babe and Man are lacking and she strides unclaimed to
    claim
Her right as femme (and baron), her equipment is the same.

She is wedded to convictions—in default of grosser ties;
Her contentions are her children, Heaven help him who denies!—
He will meet no suave discussion, but the instant, white-hot, wild,
Wakened female of the species warring as for spouse and child.

Unprovoked and awful charges—even so the she-bear fights,
Speech that drips, corrodes and poisons—even so the cobra bites,
Scientific vivisection of one nerve till it is raw
And the victim writhes in anguish—like the Jesuit with the squaw!

So it comes that Man, the coward, when he gathers to confer
With his fellow-braves in council, dare not leave a place for her

Where, at war with Life and Conscience, he uplifts his erring hands
To some God of Abstract Justice—which no woman understands.

And Man knows it! Knows, moreover, that the Woman that God
   gave him
Must command but may not govern—shall enthral but not enslave
   him.
And *She* knows, because She warns him, and Her instincts never
   fail,
That the Female of Her Species is more deadly than the Male.

The 'Mary Gloster'

I've paid for your sickest fancies; I've humoured your crackedest
  whim—
Dick, it's your daddy, dying; you've got to listen to him!
Good for a fortnight, am I? The doctor told you? He lied.
I shall go under by morning, and—Put that nurse outside.
Never seen death yet, Dickie? Well, now is your time to learn,
And you'll wish you held my record before it comes to your turn.
Not counting the Line and the Foundry, the Yards and the village,
  too,
I've made myself and a million; but I'm damned if I made you.
Master at two-and-twenty, and married at twenty-three—
Ten thousand men on the pay-roll, and forty freighters at sea!
Fifty years between 'em, and every year of it fight,
And now I'm Sir Anthony Gloster, dying, a baronite:
For I lunched with his Royal 'Ighness—what was it the papers a-
  had?
'Not least of our merchant-princes.' Dickie, that's me, your dad!
I didn't begin with askings. *I* took my job and I stuck;
I took the chances they wouldn't, an' now they're calling it luck.
Lord, what boats I've handled—rotten and leaky and old—
Ran 'em, or—opened the bilge-cock, precisely as I was told.
Grub that 'ud bind you crazy, and crews that 'ud turn you grey,
And a big fat lump of insurance to cover the risk on the way.
The others they dursn't do it; they said they valued their life
(They've served me since as skippers). *I* went, and I took my wife.
Over the world I drove 'em, married at twenty-three,
And your mother saving the money and making a man of me.
I was content to be master, but she said there was better behind;

90

She took the chances I wouldn't, and I followed your mother blind.
She egged me to borrow the money, an' she helped me to clear the
    loan,
When we bought half-shares in a cheap 'un and hoisted a flag of
    our own.
Patching and coaling on credit, and living the Lord knew how,
    We started the Red Ox freighters—we've eight-and-thirty now.
And those were the days of clippers, and the freights were clipper-
    freights,
And we knew we were making our fortune, but she died in
    Macassar Straits—
By the Little Paternosters, as you come to the Union Bank—
And we dropped her in fourteen fathom: I pricked it off where she
    sank.
Owners we were, full owners, and the boat was christened for her,
And she died in the *Mary Gloster*. My heart, how young we were!
So I went on a spree round Java and well-nigh ran ashore,
But your mother came and warned me and I wouldn't liquor no
    more:
Strict I stuck to my business, afraid to stop or I'd think,
Saving the money (she warned me), and letting the other men
    drink.
And I met M'Cullough in London (I'd turned five 'undred then),
And 'tween us we started the Foundry—three forges and twenty
    men.
Cheap repairs for the cheap 'uns. It paid, and the business grew;
For I bought me a steam-lathe patent, and that was a gold mine too.
'Cheaper to build 'em than buy 'em,' I said, but M'Cullough he
    shied,
And we wasted a year in talking before we moved to the Clyde.
And the Lines were all beginning, and we all of us started fair,
Building our engines like houses and staying the boilers square.
But M'Cullough 'e wanted cabins with marble and maple and all,
And Brussels an' Utrecht velvet, and baths and a Social Hall,
And pipes for closets all over, and cutting the frames too light,

But M'Cullough he died in the Sixties, and—Well, I'm dying to-
night . . .
I knew—I knew what was coming, when we bid on the *Byfleet's*
keel—
They piddled and piffled with iron. I'd given my orders for steel!
Steel and the fast expansions. It paid, I tell you, it paid,
When we came with our nine-knot freighters and collared the
long-run trade!
And they asked me how I did it, and I gave 'em the Scripture text,
'You keep your light so shining a little in front o' the next!'
They copied all they could follow, but they couldn't copy my mind,
And I left 'em sweating and stealing a year and a half behind.
Then came the armour-contracts, but that was M'Cullough's side;
He was always best in the Foundry, but better, perhaps, he died.
I went through his private papers; the notes was plainer than print;
And I'm no fool to finish if a man'll give me a hint.
(I remember his widow was angry.) So I saw what his drawings
meant,
And I started the six-inch rollers, and it paid me sixty per cent.
Sixty per cent *with* failures, and more than twice we could do,
And a quarter-million to credit, and I saved it all for you!
I thought—it doesn't matter—you seemed to favour your ma,
But you're nearer forty than thirty, and I know the kind you are.
Harrer an' Trinity College! I ought to ha' sent you to sea—
But I stood you an education, an' what have you done for me?
The things I knew was proper you wouldn't thank me to give,
And the things I knew was rotten you said was the way to live.
For you muddled with books and pictures, an' china an' etchin's an'
fans,
And your rooms at college was beastly—more like a whore's than a
man's;
Till you married that thin-flanked woman, as white and as stale as a
bone,
An' she gave you your social nonsense; but where's that kid o' your
own?

I've seen your carriages blocking the half o' the Cromwell Road,
But never the doctor's brougham to help the missus unload.
(So there isn't even a grandchild, an' the Gloster family's done.)
Not like your mother, she isn't. *She* carried her freight each run.
But they died, the pore little beggars! At sea she had 'em—they
    died.
Only you, an' you stood it. You haven't stood much beside.
Weak, a liar, and idle, and mean as a collier's whelp
Nosing for scraps in the galley. No help—my son was no help!
So he gets three 'undred thousand, in trust and the interest paid.
I wouldn't give it you, Dickie—you see, I made it in trade.
You're saved from soiling your fingers, and if you have no child,
It all comes back to the business. 'Gad, won't your wife be wild!
'Calls and calls in her carriage, her 'andkerchief up to 'er eye:
'Daddy! dear daddy's dyin'!' and doing her best to cry.
Grateful? Oh, yes, I'm grateful, but keep her away from here.
Your mother 'ud never ha' stood 'er, and, anyhow, women are
    queer . . .
There's women will say I've married a second time! Not quite!
But give pore Aggie a hundred, and tell her your lawyers'll fight.
She was the best o' the boiling—you'll meet her before it ends.
I'm in for a row with the mother—I'll leave you settle my friends.
For a man he must go with a woman, which women don't
    understand—
Or the sort that say they can see it they aren't the marrying brand.
But I wanted to speak o' your mother that's Lady Gloster still—
I'm going to up and see her, without it's hurting the will.
      Here! Take your hand off the bell-pull. Five thousand's
      waiting for you,
If you'll only listen a minute, and do as I bid you do.
They'll try to prove me crazy, and, if you bungle, they can;
And I've only you to trust to! (O God, why ain't he a man?)
There's some waste money on marbles, the same as M'Cullough
    tried—
Marbles and mausoleums—but I call that sinful pride.

There's some ship bodies for burial—we've carried 'em, soldered
    and packed;
Down in their wills they wrote it, and nobody called *them* cracked.
But me—I've too much money, and people might . . . All my fault:
It came o' hoping for grandsons and buying that Wokin' vault . . .
I'm sick o' the 'ole dam' business. I'm going back where I came.
Dick, you're the son o' my body, and you'll take charge o' the same!
I want to lie by your mother, ten thousand mile away,
And they'll want to send me to Woking; and that's where you'll
    earn your pay.
I've thought it out on the quiet, the same as it ought to be done—
Quiet, and decent, and proper—an' here's your orders, my son.
You know the Line? You don't, though. You write to the Board, and
    tell
Your father's death has upset you an' you're goin' to cruise for a
    spell,
An' you'd like the *Mary Gloster*—I've held her ready for this—
They'll put her in working order and you'll take her out as she is.
Yes, it was money idle when I patched her and put her aside
(Thank God, I can pay for my fancies!)—the boat where your
    mother died.
By the Little Paternosters, as you come to the Union Bank,
We dropped her—I think I told you—and I pricked it off where she
    sank,
(Tiny she looked on the grating—that oily, treacly sea—)
'Hundred and Eighteen East, remember, and South just Three.
Easy bearings to carry—Three South—Three to the dot;
But I gave M'Andrew a copy in case of dying—or not.
And so you'll write to M'Andrew, he's Chief of the Maori Line;
They'll give him leave, if you ask 'em and say it's business o' mine.
I built three boats for the Maoris, an' very well pleased they were,
An' I've known Mac since the Fifties, and Mac knew me—and her.
After the first stroke warned me I sent him the money to keep
Against the time you'd claim it, committin' your dad to the deep;
For you are the son o' my body, and Mac was my oldest friend,

I've never asked 'im to dinner, but he'll see it out to the end.
Stiff-necked Glasgow beggar! I've heard he's prayed for my soul,
But he couldn't lie if you paid him, and he'd starve before he stole.
He'll take the Mary in ballast—you'll find her a lively ship;
And you'll take Sir Anthony Gloster, that goes on 'is wedding-trip,
Lashed in our old deck-cabin with all three port-holes wide,
The kick o' the screw beneath him and the round blue seas outside!
Sir Anthony Gloster's carriage—our 'ouse-flag flyin' free—
Ten thousand men on the pay-roll and forty freighters at sea!
He made himself and a million, but this world is a fleetin' show,
And he'll go to the wife of 'is bosom the same as he ought to go—
By the heel of the Paternosters—there isn't a chance to mistake—
And Mac'll pay you the money as soon as the bubbles break!
Five thousand for six weeks' cruising, the staunchest freighter
        afloat,
And Mac he'll give you your bonus the minute I'm out o' the boat!
He'll take you round to Macassar, and you'll come back alone;
He knows what I want o' the Mary . . . I'll do what I please with my
        own.
Your mother 'ud call it wasteful, but I've seven-and-thirty more;
        I'll come in my private carriage and bid it wait at the door . . .
For my son 'e was never a credit: 'e muddled with books and art,
And 'e lived on Sir Anthony's money and 'e broke Sir Anthony's
        heart.
There isn't even a grandchild, and the Gloster family's done—
The only one you left me – O mother, the only one!
Harrer and Trinity College—me slavin' early an' late—
An' he thinks I'm dying crazy, and you're in Macassar Strait!
Flesh o' my flesh, my dearie, for ever an' ever amen,
That first stroke came for a warning. I ought to ha' gone to you
        then.
But—cheap repairs for a cheap 'un—the doctors said I'd do.
Mary, why didn't you warn me? I've allus heeded to you,
Excep'—I know—about women; but you are a spirit now;
An' wife, they was only women, and I was a man. That's how.

An' a man 'e must go with a woman, as you could not understand;
But I never talked 'em secrets. I paid 'em out o' hand.
Thank Gawd, I can pay for my fancies! Now what's five thousand
    to me,
For a berth off the Paternosters in the haven where I would be?
I believe in the Resurrection, if I read my Bible plain,
But I wouldn't trust 'em at Wokin'; we're safer at sea again.
For the heart it shall go with the treasure—go down to the sea in
    ships.
I'm sick of the hired women. I'll kiss my girl on her lips!
I'll be content with my fountain. I'll drink from my own well,
And the wife of my youth shall charm me—an' the rest can go to
    Hell!
(Dickie, *he* will, that's certain.) I'll lie in our standin'-bed,
An' Mac'll take her in ballast—an' she trims best by the head.
Down by the head an' sinkin', her fires are drawn and cold,
And the water's splashin' hollow on the skin of the empty hold—
Churning an' choking and chuckling, quiet and scummy and
    dark—
Full to her lower hatches and risin' steady. Hark!
That was the after-bulkhead . . . She's flooded from stem to stern
Never seen death yet, Dickie? . . . Well, now is your time to learn!

Recessional

God of our fathers, known of old,
    Lord of our far-flung battle-line,
Beneath whose awful Hand we hold
    Dominion over palm and pine—
Lord God of Hosts, be with us yet,
Lest we forget—lest we forget!

The tumult and the shouting dies;
    The captains and the kings depart:
Still stands Thine ancient sacrifice,
    An humble and a contrite heart.
Lord God of Hosts, be with us yet,
Lest we forget—lest we forget!

Far-called, our navies melt away;
    On dune and headland sinks the fire:
Lo, all our pomp of yesterday
    Is one with Nineveh and Tyre!
Judge of the Nations, spare us yet,
Lest we forget—lest we forget!

If, drunk with sight of power, we loose,
    Wild tongues that have not Thee in awe,
Such boastings as the Gentiles use,
    Or lesser breeds without the Law
Lord God of Hosts, be with us yet,
Lest we forget—lest we forget!

For heathen heart that puts her trust
   In reeking tube and iron shard,
All valiant dust that builds on dust,
   And guarding, calls not Thee to guard,
For frantic boast and foolish word—
Thy mercy on Thy People, Lord!

                Amen.

The Gods of the Copybook Headings

As I pass through my incarnations in every age and race,
I make my proper prostrations to the Gods of the Market-Place.
Peering through reverent fingers I watch them flourish and fall,
And the Gods of the Copybook Headings, I notice, outlast them all.

We were living in trees when they met us. They showed us each in
    turn
That Water would certainly wet us, as Fire would certainly burn:
But we found them lacking in Uplift, Vision and Breadth of Mind,
So we left them to teach the Gorillas while we followed the March
    of Mankind.

We moved as the Spirit listed. *They* never altered their pace,
Being neither cloud nor wind-borne like the Gods of the Market-
    Place;
But they always caught up with our progress, and presently word
    would come
That a tribe had been wiped off its icefield, or the lights had gone
    out in Rome.

With the Hopes that our World is built on they were utterly out of
    touch,
They denied that the Moon was Stilton; they denied she was even
    Dutch.
They denied that Wishes were Horses; they denied that a Pig had
    Wings.
So we worshipped the Gods of the Market Who promised these
    beautiful things.

When the Cambrian measures were forming, They promised
    perpetual peace.
They swore, if we gave them our weapons, that the wars of the
    tribes would cease.
But when we disarmed They sold us and delivered us bound to our
    foe,
And the Gods of the Copybook Headings said: 'Stick to the Devil you
    know.'

On the first Feminian Sandstones we were promised the Fuller Life
(Which started by loving our neighbour and ended by loving his
    wife)
Till our women had no more children and the men lost reason and
    faith,
And the Gods of the Copybook Headings said: 'The Wages of Sin is
    Death.'

In the Carboniferous Epoch we were promised abundance for all,
By robbing selected Peter to pay for collective Paul;
But, though we had plenty of money, there was nothing our money
    could buy,
And the Gods of the Copybook Headings said: 'If you don't work
    you die.'

Then the Gods of the Market tumbled, and their smooth-tongued
    wizards withdrew,
And the hearts of the meanest were humbled and began to believe
    it was true
That All is not Gold that Glitters, and Two and Two make Four—
And the Gods of the Copybook Headings limped up to explain it
    once more.

As it will be in the future, it was at the birth of Man—
There are only four things certain since Social Progress began—
That the Dog returns to his Vomit and the Sow returns to her Mire,

And the burnt Fool's bandaged finger goes wabbling back to the
    Fire;

And that after this is accomplished, and the brave new world
    begins
When all men are paid for existing and no man must pay for his
    sins,
As surely as Water will wet us, as surely as Fire will burn,
The Gods of the Copybook Headings with terror and slaughter
    return!

Danny Deever

'What are the bugles blowin' for?' said Files-on-Parade.
'To turn you out, to turn you out,' the Colour-Sergeant said.
'What makes you look so white, so white?' said Files-on-Parade.
'I'm dreadin' what I've got to watch,' the Colour-Sergeant said.
    For they're hangin' Danny Deever, you can hear the Dead
        March play,
    The regiment's in 'ollow square—they're hangin' him to-day;
    They've taken of his buttons off an' cut his stripes away,
    An' they're hangin' Danny Deever in the mornin'.

'What makes the rear-rank breathe so 'ard?' said Files-on-Parade.
'It's bitter cold, it's bitter cold,' the Colour-Sergeant said.
'What makes that front-rank man fall down?' said Files-on-Parade.
'A touch o' sun, a touch o' sun,' the Colour-Sergeant said.
    They are hangin' Danny Deever, they are marchin' of 'im
        round,
    They 'ave 'alted Danny Deever by 'is coffin on the ground;
    An' 'e'll swing in 'arf a minute for a sneakin' shootin'
        hound—
    O they're hangin' Danny Deever in the mornin'!

''Is cot was right-'and cot to mine,' said Files-on-Parade.
' 'E's sleepin' out an' far to-night,' the Colour-Sergeant said.
'I've drunk 'is beer a score o' times,' said Files-on-Parade.
' 'E's drinkin' bitter beer alone,' the Colour-Sergeant said.
    They are hangin' Danny Deever, you must mark 'im to 'is
        place,
    For 'e shot a comrade sleepin'—you must look 'im in the face;

Nine 'undred of 'is county an' the regiment's disgrace,
While they're hangin' Danny Deever in the mornin'.

'What's that so black agin the sun?' said Files-on-Parade.
'It's Danny fightin' 'ard for life,' the Colour-Sergeant said.
'What's that that whimpers over'ead?' said Files-on-Parade.
'It's Danny's soul that's passin' now,' the Colour-Sergeant said.
    For they're done with Danny Deever, you can 'ear the
        quickstep play,
    The regiment's in column, an' they're marchin' us away;
    Ho! the young recruits are shakin', an' they'll want their beer
        to-day,
    After hangin' Danny Deever in the mornin'!

Tommy

I went into a public-'ouse to get a pint o' beer,
The publican 'e up an' sez, 'We serve no red-coats here.'
The girls be'ind the bar they laughed an' giggled fit to die,
I outs into the street again an' to myself sez I:
    O it's Tommy this, an' Tommy that, an' 'Tommy, go away';
    But it's 'Thank you, Mister Atkins,' when the band begins to
      play—
    The band begins to play, my boys, the band begins to play,
    O it's 'Thank you, Mister Atkins,' when the band begins to play.

I went into a theatre as sober as could be,
They gave a drunk civilian room, but 'adn't none for me;
They sent me to the gallery or round the music-'alls,
But when it comes to fightin', Lord! they'll shove me in the stalls!
    For it's Tommy this, an' Tommy that, an' 'Tommy, wait outside';
    But it's 'Special train for Atkins' when the trooper's on the tide—
    The troopship's on the tide, my boys, the troopship's on the tide,
    O it's 'Special train for Atkins' when the trooper's on the tide.

Yes, makin' mock o' uniforms that guard you while you sleep
Is cheaper than them uniforms, an' they're starvation cheap;
An' hustlin' drunken soldiers when they're goin' large a bit
Is five times better business than paradin' in full kit.
    Then it's Tommy this an' Tommy that, an' 'Tommy, 'ow's yer soul?'
    But it's 'Thin red line of 'eroes' when the drums begin to roll—
    The drums begin to roll, my boys, the drums begin to roll,
    O it's 'Thin red line of 'eroes' when the drums begin to roll.

We aren't no thin red 'eroes, nor we aren't no blackguards too,
But single men in barricks, most remarkable like you;
An' if sometimes our conduck isn't all your fancy paints,
Why, single men in barricks don't grow into plaster saints;
    While it's Tommy this, an' Tommy that, an' 'Tommy, fall be'ind,'
    But it's 'Please to walk in front, sir,' when there's trouble in the
        wind—
    There's trouble in the wind, my boys, there's trouble in the wind,
    O it's 'Please to walk in front, sir,' when there's trouble in the
        wind.

You talk o' better food for us, an' schools, an' fires, an' all:
We'll wait for extry rations if you treat us rational.
Don't mess about the cook-room slops, but prove it to our face
The Widow's Uniform is not the soldier-man's disgrace.
    For it's Tommy this an' Tommy that, an' 'Chuck him out, the
        brute!'
    But it's 'Saviour of 'is country' when the guns begin to shoot;
    An' it's Tommy this, an' Tommy that, an' anything you please;
    An' Tommy ain't a bloomin' fool—you bet that Tommy sees!

The Children

[1914—18]

('The Honours of War' – A *Diversity of Creatures*)

These were our children who died for our lands; they were dear in
 our sight.
  We have only the memory left of their home-treasured sayings
  and laughter.
  The price of our loss shall be paid to our hands, not another's
  hereafter.
Neither the Alien nor Priest shall decide on it. That is our right.
  But who shall return us the children?

At the hour the Barbarian chose to disclose his pretences,
  And raged against Man, they engaged, on the breasts that they
  bared for us,
  The first felon-stroke of the sword he had long-time prepared for
  us—
Their bodies were all our defence while we wrought our defences.

They bought us anew with their blood, forbearing to blame us,
Those hours which we had not made good when the Judgment
  o'ercame us.
They believed us and perished for it. Our statecraft, our learning
Delivered them bound to the Pit and alive to the burning
Whither they mirthfully hastened as jostling for honour—
Not since her birth has our Earth seen such worth loosed upon her.

Nor was their agony brief, or once only imposed on them.
    The wounded, the war-spent, the sick received no exemption:
    Being cured they returned and endured and achieved our
        redemption,
Hopeless themselves of relief, till Death, marvelling, closed on
        them.

That flesh we had nursed from the first in all cleanness was given
To corruption unveiled and assailed by the malice of Heaven—
By the heart-shaking jests of Decay where it lolled on the wires—
To be blanched or gay-painted by fumes—to be cindered by fires—
To be senselessly tossed and retossed in stale mutilation
From crater to crater. For this we shall take expiation.
    But who shall return us our children?

Epitaphs of the War

[1914–1918]

'EQUALITY OF SACRIFICE'
A. 'I was a "have."' B. 'I was a "have-not."'
(*Together*). 'What hast thou given which I gave not?'

A SERVANT
We were together since the War began.
He was my servant—and the better man.

A SON
My son was killed while laughing at some jest. I would I knew
What it was, and it might serve me in a time when jests are few.

AN ONLY SON
I have slain none except my Mother. She
(Blessing her slayer) died of grief for me.

EX-CLERK
Pity not! The Army gave
Freedom to a timid slave:
In which Freedom did he find
Strength of body, will, and mind:
By which strength he came to prove
Mirth, Companionship, and Love:
For which Love to Death he went:
In which Death he lies content.

THE WONDER
Body and Spirit I surrendered whole
To harsh Instructors—and received a soul . . .
If mortal man could change me through and through
From all I was—what may the God not do?

HINDU SEPOY IN FRANCE
This man in his own country prayed we know not to what Powers
We pray Them to reward him for his bravery in ours.

THE COWARD
I could not look on Death, which being known,
Men led me to him, blindfold and alone.

SHOCK
My name, my speech, my self I had forgot.
My wife and children came—I knew them not.
I died. My Mother followed. At her call
And on her bosom I remembered all.

A GRAVE NEAR CAIRO
Gods of the Nile, should this stout fellow here
Get out—get out! He knows not shame nor fear.

PELICANS IN THE WILDERNESS
A Grave near Halfa
The blown sand heaps on me, that none may learn
    Where I am laid for whom my children grieve . . .
O wings that beat at dawning, ye return
    Out of the desert to your young at eve!

RUDYARD KIPLING

TWO CANADIAN MEMORIALS

I

We giving all gained all.
    Neither lament us nor praise.
Only in all things recall,
    It is Fear, not Death that slays.

II

From little towns in a far land we came,
    To save our honour and a world aflame.
By little towns in a far land we sleep;
    And trust that world we won for you to keep!

THE FAVOUR

Death favoured me from the first, well knowing I could not
    endure
    To wait on him by day by day. He quitted my betters and came
Whistling over the fields, and, when he had made all sure,
    'Thy line is at end,' he said, 'but at least I have saved its name.'

THE BEGINNER

On the first hour of my first day
    In the front trench I fell.
(Children in boxes at a play
    Stand up to watch it well.)

R.A.F. (AGED EIGHTEEN)

Laughing through clouds, his milk-teeth still unshed,
Cities and men he smote from overhead.
His deaths delivered, he returned to play
Childlike, with childish things now put away.

THE REFINED MAN

I was of delicate mind. I stepped aside for my needs,
    Disdaining the common office. I was seen from afar and killed . . .

How is this matter for mirth? Let each man be judged by his deeds.
I have paid my price to live with myself on the terms that I willed.

NATIVE WATER-CARRIER (M.E.F.)
Prometheus brought down fire to men,
   This brought up water.
The Gods are jealous—now, as then,
   They gave no quarter.

BOMBED IN LONDON
On land and sea I strove with anxious care
To escape conscription. It was in the air!

THE SLEEPY SENTINEL
Faithless the watch that I kept: now I have none to keep.
I was slain because I slept: now I am slain I sleep.
Let no man reproach me again, whatever watch is unkept—
I sleep because I am slain. They slew me because I slept.

BATTERIES OUT OF AMMUNITION
If any mourn us in the workshop, say
We died because the shift kept holiday.

COMMON FORM
If any question why we died,
Tell them, because our fathers lied.

A DEAD STATESMAN
I could not dig: I dared not rob:
Therefore I lied to please the mob.
Now all my lies are proved untrue
And I must face the men I slew.
What tale shall serve me here among
Mine angry and defrauded young?

RUDYARD KIPLING

THE REBEL

If I had clamoured at Thy Gate
    For gift of Life on Earth,
And, thrusting through the souls that wait,
    Flung headlong into birth—
Even then, even then, for gin and snare
    About my pathway spread,
Lord, I had mocked Thy thoughtful care
    Before I joined the Dead!
But now? . . . I was beneath Thy Hand
    Ere yet the Planets came.
And now—though Planets pass, I stand
    The witness to Thy Shame.

THE OBEDIENT

Daily, though no ears attended,
    Did my prayers arise.
Daily, though no fire descended,
    Did I sacrifice.
Though my darkness did not lift,
    Though I faced no lighter odds,
Though the Gods bestowed no gift,
    None the less,
None the less, I served the Gods!

A DRIFTER OFF TARENTUM

He from the wind-bitten North with ship and companions
        descended,
    Searching for eggs of death spawned by invisible hulls.
Many he found and drew forth. Of a sudden the fishery ended
    In flame and a clamorous breath not new to the eye-pecking
        gulls.

DESTROYERS IN COLLISION

For Fog and Fate no charm is found

To lighten or amend.
I, hurrying to my bride, was drowned—
    Cut down by my best friend.

CONVOY ESCORT

I was a shepherd to fools
    Causelessly bold or afraid.
They would not abide by my rules.
    Yet they escaped. For I stayed.

UNKNOWN FEMALE CORPSE

Headless, lacking foot and hand,
Horrible I come to land.
I beseech all women's sons
Know I was a mother once.

RAPED AND AVENGED

One used and butchered me: another spied
Me broken—for which thing an hundred died.
So it was learned among the heathen hosts
How much a freeborn woman's favour costs.

SALONIKAN GRAVE

I have watched a thousand days
Push out and crawl into night
Slowly as tortoises.
Now I, too, follow these.
It is fever, and not the fight—
Time, not battle—that slays.

THE BRIDEGROOM

Call me not false, beloved,
    If, from thy scarce-known breast
So little time removed,
    In other arms I rest.

For this more ancient bride,
   Whom coldly I embrace,
Was constant at my side
   Before I saw thy face.

Our marriage, often set—
   By miracle delayed—
At last is consummate,
   And cannot be unmade.

Live, then, whom Life shall cure,
   Almost, of Memory,
And leave us to endure
   Its immortality.

V.A.D. (MEDITERRANEAN)

Ah, would swift ships had never been, for then we ne'er had found,
These harsh Aegean rocks between, this little virgin drowned,
Whom neither spouse nor child shall morn, but men she nursed
     through pain
And—certain keels for whose return the heathen look in vain.

ACTORS

On a Memorial Tablet in Holy Trinity Church,
Stratford-on-Avon

We counterfeited once for your disport
   Men's joy and sorrow: but our day has passed.
We pray you pardon all where we fell short—
   Seeing we were your servants to this last.

JOURNALISTS
On a Panel in the Hall of the Institute of Journalists

We have served our day.

PHILIP LARKIN

Philip Arthur Larkin was born in Coventry in 1922. A poet, novelist and librarian, his publication of *The Whitsun Weddings* (1964) and *High Windows* (1974) secured his reputation. He refused the position of Poet Laureate in 1984 but accepted the Order of The Companion of Honour in 1985, the year of his death.

PHILIP LARKIN

Too Clever to Live?

In 1984 I approached Philip Larkin to request permission to present an evening of his poetry read by Alan Bates. Though warned by his old friend Kingsley Amis, 'Oh dear, no, Josephine, Philip won't like this at all,' I persevered. Mr Larkin said yes. I sent him roses after the reading. In his letter of thanks Philip Larkin described the arrival of the bouquet at reception in Hull Library, where he worked as Chief Librarian, its procession from department to department, the tentative smiles of hope that faded as, impervious to silent entreaties of 'Let it be me,' the arrangement was eventually handed to him. In subject matter, that letter could easily have been a Larkin poem, illustrating as it did a key motif in his poetry: the significance of small events and their defining pressure on individual psychology, most particularly his own. An invitation to a drinks party, a visit to an empty church, a recently vacated room in a boarding house: such everyday events are transmuted by Larkin into poetry that gives weight to the ordinary dreams and fears of our daily lives, lived out as they are in the shadow of eternity. We recognize ourselves in his poems, as we do in a Chekhov play, and we smile and our smiles are rueful.

'I like to read about people who have done nothing spectacular, aren't beautiful or lucky; who try to behave well in a limited field of activity and who can see in the little autumnal moments of vision that the so called "big experiences of life" are going to miss them. I like to read about such things presented not with self-pity or despair or romanticism but with realistic firmness and even humour.' This, Larkin wrote, was the 'moral tone' of Barbara Pym's novels. It is also the moral tone of much of Larkin's work. He believed art should help us either to 'enjoy or endure'. Yet he himself seemed to find neither enjoyment nor endurance easy. Though he was an adored child from a secure middle-class background, tensions in his parents' marriage and the hushed atmosphere in his house may have inspired the sad line, 'What was the rock my gliding childhood struck?'

His parents, Sydney Larkin OBE, and his bookish wife, Eva, encouraged his literary interests and were in fact hugely proud of him. His life was crowned with success. He sailed into Oxford and sailed out again, a published poet, and to his delight, with a first-class honours degree. Shortly after Oxford he published two novels, *Jill* and *A Girl in Winter*, became a professional librarian, combining the roles of scholar, curator and administrator in an exemplary career. His *Who's Who* entry states his occupation as Librarian: 'A man *is* what he is paid for.' His four collections of poetry, *The Less Deceived*, *High Windows*, *The North Ship* and *The Whitsun Weddings*, made him one of the most acclaimed English poets of the twentieth century. He won the Gold Medal for Poetry and was offered, but turned down, the poet laureateship; 'Poetry, that rare bird, has flown out of the window.' In his private life he was a much loved man. Andrew Motion in his biography, *Philip Larkin, A Writer's Life*, charts a course with great elegance through not only the development of the poet but also the labyrinthine ways of Larkin and his women. He makes clear that two women – in particular, Monica Jones and Maeve Brennan – loved him for decades and that there were other, serious relationships. It would seem that Larkin inspired in women levels of self-sacrifice that would have done Byron proud. Ironically, one of his most quoted lines is: 'What will survive of us is love.'

Was he, however, just 'too clever to live'? The question is posed by A. L. Rowse, whose library edition of Larkin's *Required Writing* I had the good luck to buy, containing, as it does, challenging, handwritten comments on virtually every page: 'Kindly face, no kidding him', 'perverse psychology, Irish perhaps?' But it wasn't just cleverness that made Larkin 'miss out on the big experiences of life'. The 'deprivation', which was to him 'what daffodils were to Wordsworth', was, in his case, elective. The 'examined life' led to a life at bay.

Why? For art's sake? It would seem so. His long dialogue with self, 'Self's the Man' (the title of one of his poems), is a battleground between art and life. 'When I think of being in my *twenties* or even my *thirties*, my external surroundings have changed but inside I've been the same, trying to hold everything off in order to write.' It wasn't just Cyril Connolly's enemy of promise, 'the pram in the hall', that Larkin feared; it was the hall, the kitchen, the sitting room, if they contained people with claims on the time in his life. No poet ever feared the end of his time more than Philip Larkin. In the brutal choice for all artists – and not only artists – of 'perfection of the work rather than of the life' (Yeats's haunting phrase), Larkin came down firmly, knowingly, on the side of art. If at the end of her monologue Joyce's Molly Bloom sounds the most emphatic yes in literature (and in plural), Larkin's poems move inexorably to an emphatic no. In Christopher Ricks's brilliant insight, 'Just as a romantic swell of feeling rises' it meets 'a counter thrust of classical impersonality,' we have the essence of that tension that makes Larkin's poems so thrilling to read.

Larkin sets you down immediately, with almost cinematic exactitude, in the 'scene', and as Alan Bennett notes, 'He still has you firmly by the hand as you cross the finishing line.' And Larkin's finishing lines are pure gold. Last lines are 'the stamp', as John Donne wrote, that authenticate what great poetry is – in itself 'the beating out of a piece of gold'. With Larkin, the poetic journey may be short, the image fleeting; there may be stops along the way (interrupted journeys are a recurrent theme); but at the point of arrival we know the place. Perhaps we've been there before. Larkin's round-life trips are more challenging than any round-the-world trip. He knows the great adventure is internal. The man whose voice, as Andrew Motion noted, is 'one of the means by which his country recognises itself', did not travel far, even in England. He was born in Coventry in 1922. He died in Hull in 1985. 'I am going to the inevitable.' No Kipling, he.

His own divine comedy was not set in the middle of a dark wood 'but in a railway tunnel, half way through England' as Seamus Heaney said as he listened, as we all do, to Larkin's 'un-foolable mind . . . singing the melody of intelligence'.

The Poems

'He is the only sophisticated poet today who requires no sophisticated response from the reader,' John Bayley wrote in 1983. Twenty-three years later and long after Larkin's death, Bayley's insight remains true. Larkin once observed that he'd found a way of 'making novels into poems'. Intriguingly, it was a novelist turned poet, Thomas Hardy, who killed Larkin's early obsession with the music of Yeats – 'as pervasive as garlic' in Larkin's later description. As in many novels resolution is sudden. The rejection in 'Poetry of Departures' to the elemental dream of leaving comes just as the heart quickens with the exhilaration of *He chucked up everything/And just cleared off* to 'swagger the nut-strewn roads', or 'Crouch in the fo'c'sle/Stubbly with goodness,'. Then, suddenly, the race is over before it has started.

In 'I Remember, I Remember' Larkin reminds us that we all start from home, the memory of which never leaves us. The train stops at Coventry, the station sign becoming the Proustian 'madeleine' that inspires memories of 'where my childhood was unspent', of 'The bracken where I never trembling sat . . . where she/Lay back, and 'all became a burning mist'. The witty truth of most childhoods tumbles down to one of the great last lines in poetry: 'Nothing, like something, happens anywhere.' Proust, subverted. It's hard to get away from nothing. Larkin once described the difficulty in escaping from home as akin to 'writing *Decline and Fall of the Roman Empire.*'

In 'This Be The Verse' there is gender equality in the parental blame game. Nature and nurture fail. Perhaps Beckett is right, 'Never to have been born is best.' After all, 'They fuck you up, your mum and dad.' Larkin, in a letter to Kingsley Amis, said of the poem, 'Clearly my Lake Isle of Innisfree. I fully expect to hear it recited by a 1000 Girl Guides before I die.' What an excellent idea! Also for boy scouts.

Parental guilt removed at a stroke. The last lines are an exercise in exuberant nihilism: 'Get out as early as you can/And don't have any kids yourself.'

'Vers de Société' is Larkin's version of Sartre's 'Hell is other people'. He once said, 'I see life more as an affair of solitude diversified by company than an affair of company diversified by solitude.' The reason is deeper than unsociability. Parties to Larkin are the waste of precious time that would be better 'repaid/Under a lamp, hearing the noise of wind/And looking out to see the moon thinned/To an air-sharpened blade.'

'Mr Bleaney' is a dialogue with a ghost. What do we leave behind us in the rooms we have vacated? Or in the life we have vacated 'which measures our own nature'? Was Mr Bleaney satisfied 'at his age having no more to show/Than one hired box'? Perhaps 'He warranted no better, I don't know'. Who knows?

'Church Going' explores reverence without religion, in an empty church actually in Ireland. The 'unignorable silence' into which the accumulated ceremonies of life and death echo in 'A serious house on serious earth' which is 'proper to grow wise in,/If only that so many dead lie round'. Definitely Ireland.

'The Whitsun Weddings' is a Fellini-like vision on station platforms of 'grinning and pomaded, girls/In parodies of fashion, heels and veils/ . . . The fathers with broad belts under their suits/ . . . mothers loud and fat' as 'A dozen marriages got under way/ . . . with all the power/That being changed can give.'

The Dickensian title of 'Dockery and Son' is apt. It's my favourite Larkin poem, a novel of a poem. Larkin always wanted to be a novelist and believed that 'poetry chose me', luckily for us. The poem is about youth and what one does with it. Dockery is remembered by the wifeless, childless, middle-aged narrator as a boy who seized his moment sexually and begot a son, who now attends their old college. Then, provocatively, Larkin throws down the philosophical gauntlet: 'Why did he [Dockery] think adding meant increase?/ . . .Where do these/Innate assumptions come from?' One of the great questions. One of the great poems.

Poetry of Departures

Sometimes you hear, fifth-hand,
As epitaph:
He chucked up everything
And just cleared off,
And always the voice will sound
Certain you approve
This audacious, purifying,
Elemental move.

And they are right, I think.
We all hate home
And having to be there:
I detest my room,
Its specially-chosen junk,
The good books, the good bed,
And my life, in perfect order:
So to hear it said

He walked out on the whole crowd
Leaves me flushed and stirred,
Like *Then she undid her dress*
Or *Take that you bastard;*
Surely I can, if he did?
And that helps me stay
Sober and industrious.
But I'd go today,

Yes, swagger the nut-strewn roads,
Crouch in the fo'c'sle

Stubbly with goodness, if
It weren't so artificial,
Such a deliberate step backwards
To create an object:
Books; china; a life
Reprehensibly perfect.

I Remember, I Remember

Coming up England by a different line
For once, early in the cold new year,
We stopped, and, watching men with number-plates
Sprint down the platform to familiar gates,
'Why, Coventry!' I exclaimed. 'I was born here.'

I leant far out, and squinnied for a sign
That this was still the town that had been 'mine'
So long, but found I wasn't even clear
Which side was which. From where those cycle-crates
Were standing, had we annually departed

For all those family hols? . . . A whistle went:
Things moved. I sat back, staring at my boots.
'Was that,' my friend smiled, 'where you "have your roots"?'
No, only where my childhood was unspent,
I wanted to retort, just where I started:

By now I've got the whole place clearly charted.
Our garden, first: where I did not invent
Blinding theologies of flowers and fruits,
And wasn't spoken to by an old hat.
And here we have that splendid family

I never ran to when I got depressed,
The boys all biceps and the girls all chest,
Their comic Ford, their farm where I could be
'Really myself'. I'll show you, come to that,
The bracken where I never trembling sat,

Determined to go through with it; where she
Lay back, and 'all became a burning mist'.
And, in those offices, my doggerel
Was not set up in blunt ten-point, nor read
By a distinguished cousin of the mayor,

Who didn't call and tell my father *There
Before us, had we the gift to see ahead* –
'You look as if you wished the place in Hell,'
My friend said, 'judging from your face.' 'Oh well,
I suppose it's not the place's fault,' I said.

'Nothing, like something, happens anywhere.'

This Be The Verse

They fuck you up, your mum and dad.
   They may not mean to, but they do.
They fill you with the faults they had
   And add some extra, just for you.

But they were fucked up in their turn
   By fools in old-style hats and coats,
Who half the time were soppy-stern
   And half at one another's throats.

Man hands on misery to man.
   It deepens like a coastal shelf.
Get out as early as you can,
   And don't have any kids yourself.

Vers de Société

My wife and I have asked a crowd of craps
To come and waste their time and ours: perhaps
You'd care to join us? In a pig's arse, friend.
Day comes to an end.
The gas fire breathes, the trees are darkly swayed.
And so Dear Warlock-Williams: I'm afraid –

Funny how hard it is to be alone.
I could spend half my evenings, if I wanted,
Holding a glass of washing sherry, canted
Over to catch the drivel of some bitch
Who's read nothing but Which;
Just think of all the spare time that has flown

Straight into nothingness by being filled
With forks and faces, rather than repaid
Under a lamp, hearing the noise of wind,
And looking out to see the moon thinned
To an air-sharpened blade.
A life, and yet how sternly it's instilled

All solitude is selfish. No one now
Believes the hermit with his gown and dish
Talking to God (who's gone too); the big wish
Is to have people nice to you, which means
Doing it back somehow.
Virtue is social. Are, then, these routines

Playing at goodness, like going to church?
Something that bores us, something we don't do well
(Asking that ass about his fool research)
But try to feel, because, however crudely,
It shows us what should be?
Too subtle, that. Too decent, too. Oh hell,

Only the young can be alone freely.
The time is shorter now for company,
And sitting by a lamp more often brings
Not peace, but other things.
Beyond the light stand failure and remorse
Whispering *Dear Warlock-Williams: Why, of course —*

Mr Bleaney

'This was Mr Bleaney's room. He stayed
The whole time he was at the Bodies, till
They moved him.' Flowered curtains, thin and frayed,
Fall to within five inches of the sill,

Whose window shows a strip of building land,
Tussocky, littered. 'Mr Bleaney took
My bit of garden properly in hand.'
Bed, upright chair, sixty-watt bulb, no hook

Behind the door, no room for books or bags –
'I'll take it.' So it happens that I lie
Where Mr Bleaney lay, and stub my fags
On the same saucer-souvenir, and try

Stuffing my ears with cotton-wool, to drown
The jabbering set he egged her on to buy.
I know his habits – what time he came down,
His preference for sauce to gravy, why

He kept on plugging at the four aways –
Likewise their yearly frame: the Frinton folk
Who put him up for summer holidays,
And Christmas at his sister's house in Stoke.

But if he stood and watched the frigid wind
Tousling the clouds, lay on the fusty bed
Telling himself that this was home, and grinned,
And shivered, without shaking off the dread

That how we live measures our own nature,
And at his age having no more to show
Than one hired box should make him pretty sure
He warranted no better, I don't know.

Church Going

Once I am sure there's nothing going on
I step inside, letting the door thud shut.
Another church: matting, seats, and stone,
And little books; sprawlings of flowers, cut
For Sunday, brownish now; some brass and stuff
Up at the holy end; the small neat organ;
And a tense, musty, unignorable silence,
Brewed God knows how long. Hatless, I take off
My cycle-clips in awkward reverence,

Move forward, run my hand around the font.
From where I stand, the roof looks almost new –
Cleaned, or restored? Someone would know: I don't.
Mounting the lectern, I peruse a few
Hectoring large-scale verses, and pronounce
'Here endeth' much more loudly than I'd meant.
The echoes snigger briefly. Back at the door
I sign the book, donate an Irish sixpence,
Reflect the place was not worth stopping for.

Yet stop I did: in fact I often do,
And always end much at a loss like this,
Wondering what to look for; wondering, too,
When churches fall completely out of use
What we shall turn them into, if we shall keep
A few cathedrals chronically on show,
Their parchment, plate and pyx in locked cases,

And let the rest rent-free to rain and sheep.
Shall we avoid them as unlucky places?

Or, after dark, will dubious women come
To make their children touch a particular stone;
Pick simples for a cancer; or on some
Advised night see walking a dead one?
Power of some sort or other will go on
In games, in riddles, seemingly at random;
But superstition, like belief, must die,
And what remains when disbelief has gone?
Grass, weedy pavement, brambles, buttress, sky,

A shape less recognisable each week,
A purpose more obscure. I wonder who
Will be the last, the very last, to seek
This place for what it was; one of the crew
That tap and jot and know what rood-lofts were?
Some ruin-bibber, randy for antique,
Or Christmas-addict, counting on a whiff
Of gown-and-bands and organ-pipes and myrrh?
Or will he be my representative,

Bored, uninformed, knowing the ghostly silt
Dispersed, yet tending to this cross of ground
Through suburb scrub because it held unspilt
So long and equably what since is found
Only in separation – marriage, and birth,
And death, and thoughts of these – for which was built
This special shell? For, though I've no idea
What this accoutred frowsty barn is worth,
It pleases me to stand in silence here;

A serious house on serious earth it is,
In whose blent air all our compulsions meet,

Are recognised, and robed as destinies.
And that much never can be obsolete,
Since someone will forever be surprising
A hunger in himself to be more serious,
And gravitating with it to this ground,
Which, he once heard, was proper to grow wise in,
If only that so many dead lie round.

The Whitsun Weddings

That Whitsun, I was late getting away:
  Not till about
One-twenty on the sunlit Saturday
Did my three-quarters-empty train pull out,
All windows down, all cushions hot, all sense
Of being in a hurry gone. We ran
Behind the backs of houses, crossed a street
Of blinding windscreens, smelt the fish-dock; thence
The river's level drifting breadth began,
Where sky and Lincolnshire and water meet.

All afternoon, through the tall heat that slept
  For miles inland,
A slow and stopping curve southwards we kept.
Wide farms went by, short-shadowed cattle, and
Canals with floatings of industrial froth;
A hothouse flashed uniquely: hedges dipped
And rose: and now and then a smell of grass
Displaced the reek of buttoned carriage-cloth
Until the next town, new and nondescript,
Approached with acres of dismantled cars.

At first, I didn't notice what a noise
  The weddings made
Each station that we stopped at: sun destroys
The interest of what's happening in the shade,
And down the long cool platforms whoops and skirls
I took for porters larking with the mails,

And went on reading. Once we started, though,
We passed them, grinning and pomaded, girls
In parodies of fashion, heels and veils,
All posed irresolutely, watching us go,

As if out on the end of an event
    Waving goodbye
To something that survived it. Struck, I leant
More promptly out next time, more curiously,
And saw it all again in different terms:
The fathers with broad belts under their suits
And seamy foreheads; mothers loud and fat;
An uncle shouting smut; and then the perms,
The nylon gloves and jewellery-substitutes,
The lemons, mauves, and olive-ochres that

Marked off the girls unreally from the rest.
    Yes, from cafés
And banquet-halls up yards, and bunting-dressed
Coach-party annexes, the wedding-days
Were coming to an end. All down the line
Fresh couples climbed aboard: the rest stood round;
The last confetti and advice were thrown,
And, as we moved, each face seemed to define
Just what it saw departing: children frowned
At something dull; fathers had never known

Success so huge and wholly farcical;
    The women shared
The secret like a happy funeral;
While girls, gripping their handbags tighter, stared
At a religious wounding. Free at last,
And loaded with the sum of all they saw,
We hurried towards London, shuffling gouts of steam.
Now fields were building-plots, and poplars cast

Long shadows over major roads, and for
Some fifty minutes, that in time would seem

Just long enough to settle hats and say
    I nearly died,
A dozen marriages got under way.
They watched the landscape, sitting side by side
– An Odeon went past, a cooling tower,
And someone running up to bowl – and none
Thought of the others they would never meet
Or how their lives would all contain this hour.
I thought of London spread out in the sun,
Its postal districts packed like squares of wheat:

There we were aimed. And as we raced across
    Bright knots of rail
Past standing Pullmans, walls of blackened moss
Came close, and it was nearly done, this frail
Travelling coincidence; and what it held
Stood ready to be loosed with all the power
That being changed can give. We slowed again,
And as the tightened brakes took hold, there swelled
A sense of falling, like an arrow-shower
Sent out of sight, somewhere becoming rain.

Dockery and Son

'Dockery was junior to you,
Wasn't he?' said the Dean. 'His son's here now.'
Death-suited, visitant, I nod. 'And do
You keep in touch with –' Or remember how
Black-gowned, unbreakfasted, and still half-tight
We used to stand before that desk, to give
'Our version' of 'these incidents last night'?
I try the door of where I used to live:

Locked. The lawn spreads dazzlingly wide.
A known bell chimes. I catch my train, ignored.
Canal and clouds and colleges subside
Slowly from view. But Dockery, good Lord,
Anyone up today must have been born
In '43, when I was twenty-one.
If he was younger, did he get this son
At nineteen, twenty? Was he that withdrawn

High-collared public-schoolboy, sharing rooms
With Cartwright who was killed? Well, it just shows
How much . . . How little . . . Yawning, I suppose
I fell asleep, waking at the fumes
And furnace-glares of Sheffield, where I changed,
And ate an awful pie, and walked along
The platform to its end to see the ranged
Joining and parting lines reflect a strong

Unhindered moon. To have no son, no wife,
No house or land still seemed quite natural.

Only a numbness registered the shock
Of finding out how much had gone of life,
How widely from the others. Dockery, now:
Only nineteen, he must have taken stock
Of what he wanted, and been capable
Of . . . No, that's not the difference: rather, how

Convinced he was he should be added to!
Why did he think adding meant increase?
To me it was dilution. Where do these
Innate assumptions come from? Not from what
We think truest, or most want to do:
Those warp tight-shut, like doors. They're more a style
Our lives bring with them: habit for a while,
Suddenly they harden into all we've got

And how we got it; looked back on, they rear
Like sand-clouds, thick and close, embodying
For Dockery a son, for me nothing,
Nothing with all a son's harsh patronage.
Life is first boredom, then fear.
Whether or not we use it, it goes,
And leaves what something hidden from us chose,
And age, and then the only end of age.

MARIANNE MOORE

Born in 1887 in Kirkwood, Missouri, Marianne Craig
Moore was a poet, essayist and translator. Her *Selected
Poems* (1935) was published with an introduction by T. S.
Eliot. She won both the Gold Medal for Poetry from the
American Academy of Arts and Letters and the Pulitzer
Prize. She died in 1972.

MARIANNE MOORE

Poetry . . . I, Too, Dislike It

'I like country fairs, roller-coasters, merry-go-rounds, dog shows, museums, avenues of trees, old elms, vehicles' (on being asked to name the new Ford she suggested 'the utopian turtle top' or 'the intelligent whale'), 'experiments in timing, like our ex-Museum of Science and Invention's two roller-bearings in a gravity chute, synchronized with a ring-bearing, revolving vertically. I am fond of animals and take inordinate interest in mongooses, squirrels, crows, elephants.' This is Marianne Moore on Marianne Moore, one of the 'Authors of 1951 Speaking for Themselves' in the *New York Herald Tribune*. She also listed as among the few great artists of her time Casals, Soledad, Alec Guinness and the Lipizzaner horsemen. She adored gardenias, beautiful clothes, Beatrix Potter and baseball, which she compared to writing. She told *Esquire* in 1962 that she regarded the statement by a famous player that 'Marianne Moore speaks to our condition as ballplayers' as one of the great compliments of her life. She wrote the liner notes to Muhammad Ali's TV series, 'I Am the Greatest'. Though she never married, lived quietly at home and was an inveterate letter writer, Emily Dickinson she is not.

Neither love ('My Senses Do Not Deceive Me') nor death are primarily her subjects, nor does time feature greatly. Art gets more attention, as does war, the pangolin, roses, monkeys, snails, steamrollers and that most fascinating subject, human behaviour. She is cool. She is thrilling. Despite the fact that Hilda Doolittle first published Moore (without her permission); that she became a mentor to

Elizabeth Bishop; that Grace Schulman edited the current Faber collection, nevertheless she may have found her precursors were men rather than women, according to Cynthia Hogan. And the men found her. 'Miss Moore's poetry forms part of the small body of durable poetry written in our time . . . in which an original sensibility and alert intelligence and deep feeling have been engaged in maintaining the life of the English language': T. S. Eliot in his preface to *Selected Writings by Marianne Moore*. W. H. Auden said of her, 'Marianne Moore is one of the very few modern-day poets I can read any day, or in any mood.' She numbered fellow poets William Carlos Williams and Randall Jarrell among her admirers. She won the Bollingen Prize, the National Book Award, the Pulitzer Prize and, for her translation of the fables of La Fontaine – a work that took her over ten years to complete – the coveted Croix de Chevalier des Arts et Lettres.

'The Mind Is an Enchanting Thing,' she wrote. Marianne Moore's mind enchants us with its truthfulness, its clarity, its wit. For once, the word 'rapier-like' is legitimate. 'If Miss Moore is laughing at us, it is laughter that catches us . . . and half-paralyses us, as light flashed from a very fine steel blade, wielded playfully, ironically . . . Yet with all that craftsmanship . . . her art resides only in that serene palace of her own world of inspiration – frail, yet as all beautiful things are, absolutely hard': Hilda Doolittle in her essay on Moore for *The Egoist* – the short-lived but immensely influential literary journal. Her art is also direct. There is with other poets, and particularly Dickinson, the delight in the thing seen 'slant'. That is not where delight is found in Marianne Moore. Though she is intellectually complex, the fresh-washed quality of her work comes from the 'straight on' vision. She sees 'the rock crystal thing to see'. She is, as Randall Jarrell said of her in his essay 'Her Shield', 'the poet of the particular'. The particular, and the demand that it be described accurately, was key to the aesthetic philosophy with which she is associated: imagism. 'The natural object is always the adequate symbol' was Ezra Pound's mantra. (Pound was, it seems, everywhere.) Grace Schulman points out that her laboratory studies affected Moore's poetry profoundly. 'Art is exact perception' is the opening line of one of her poems 'And no man who's done his part/Need apologize for art.'

She did not write poetry 'for money or fame. To earn a living is needful, but it can be done in routine ways. One writes because one has a burning desire to objectify what it is indispensable to one's happiness to express.' 'Objectify' is the operative word in that sentence. In her poetry, which she once referred to as Escher compositions, each word is precisely positioned on the page, though not necessarily in the precise position one might expect! Moore was, as Grace Schulman notes, often irritated by those who commented upon the strict syllabic method from which she did not deviate. However, its accommodation – which necessitated the regular splitting of words from line to line – is fundamental to the structure of her work and its Pound-like visual effect on the page. Later in life, however, she was to say to Schulman that the sound of her poetry was more important to her than its visual effect on the page.

The visual effect is nevertheless powerful – but always to a purpose, for example, her generous use of inverted commas around every borrowed or stolen line, even from dinner party guests. When asked why, she said, 'When a thing has been said so well that it could not be said better, why paraphrase it? Hence my writing is, if not a cabinet of fossils, a kind of collection of flies in amber.' Thus one learns to trust her. It is strange how compelling that reaction becomes, as one begins to see clearly what Auden saw: 'with what unfreckled integrity it has all been done'.

The seeds of that integrity were sown early. Until she was seven Marianne Moore lived in the home of her grandfather, a Presbyterian pastor. Her father, over whose mental health there seems to have been a shadow, disappeared shortly before her birth – she was never to meet him. She attended Bryn Mawr. In her introduction to *Selected Letters*, and there were thousands from which one could select, Bonnie Costello quotes a line of rather daunting self-knowledge from a letter to a friend: 'My experience [at Bryn Mawr] gave me security in my determination to have what I want.' Commercial college in Carlisle, Pennsylvania, followed, where she studied typing and business, which she then taught, evidently extremely well. In 1918 when she was thirty-one Marianne Moore moved to New York – 'the savage's romance' that gave her 'accessibility to experience'. Since she worked for the New York Public Library and later edited the prestigious *The Dial*, a literary journal, which counted Yeats, Eliot and Pound among its contributors, it also gave her accessibility to virtually every major literary figure in America. Marianne Moore's was a long and brilliant life in literature, in which the black-caped, three-corner hatted, white-haired woman became an icon of American letters.

Her very 'properness' gives a surprising salt and dash to her work. She was never for sale – to anyone. Her disciplined artist's eye looked on her own work and cut it ruthlessly. Patricia C. Willis notes in her introduction to *Marianne Moore, Woman and Poet* that the poem titled 'Poetry' once shrank from five stanzas to thirteen lines, and eventually to three lines! Luckily she relented, though as she said, 'Omissions are not accidents.' She died in 1972, aged eighty-five. Grace Schulman tells us that Ezra Pound came out of his long seclusion to recite her poem 'What are Years?' at her memorial service. The last line of the poem is appropriate to a woman who looked unflinchingly at life and its inevitable end: 'This is mortality/this is eternity.' She may have written of poetry, 'I, too, dislike it: there are things that are important beyond all this fiddle.' The poem, however, continues, 'Reading it, however, with a perfect contempt for it, one discovers in it, after all, a place for the genuine.'

The Poems

'Making, Knowing, Judging', Auden's trinity, 'an insight of casual genius' according to Heaney, seems particularly applicable to the work of Marianne Moore. And of these three virtues, with Marianne Moore, the greatest, I think, is knowing. 'The Mind Is an Enchanting Thing', one of her most brilliant poems, emblematic of her particular respect for the intellect, ends with the famous 'it's/not a Herod's oath that cannot change.' She did not, in fact, change her mind about much philosophically. She did, however, like Lowell, constantly refine and redefine her own work. Lines were often erased – silenced. 'We All Know It': 'That silence is best.' Do we? 'A strange idea that one must say what one thinks in order to be understood.'

'Silence', the title this time, opens with the conversational 'My father used say,/'Superior people never make long visits'. A remark made by a visiting professor is juxtaposed with Edmund Burke's eighteenth-century invitation to someone he'd met in a bookshop: to 'Make my house your inn.' Add Moore's coolly subversive last line and we glimpse the subtle art of being either guest or host. I would visit Miss Moore with some trepidation and would certainly try to curb the intensity with which I speak.

'To Be Liked by You Would Be a Calamity' is possibly the best put-down in poetry. Moore, evidently a brilliant conversationalist, enjoyed the elegant thrust and parry of intellectual debate. The blunt instrument of aggression, however, which aims to put 'My flesh beneath your feet', leads to a contemptuous withdrawal. She stood up *to* – that most difficult act of honour – as well as *for* her friends. Perhaps this quality was key to the great respect in which she was held by her contemporaries. It's also, perhaps, a slightly thorny quality. In 'Roses Only' the thorn garners exquisite attention – 'compelling audience to/the remark that it is better to be forgotten than to be remembered too violently,/your thorns are the best part of you.'

The clever 'I Like A Horse but I Have a Fellow Feeling for A Mule' should be treasured and not only for its title. I would guess that Moore had a stubborn streak. Guessing would no doubt meet with disapproval; she had an admirable respect for facts. Moore expresses her gratitude to the mule in measured, careful beats – like him, never going too far; 'he skirts the treeless precipice.' Moore had a 'fellow feeling' for most animals and gave each of them their due. Her masterpiece, 'The Pangolin', deserves an essay in itself. Alas!

'Spenser's Ireland' cuts to the soul of Auden's 'mad Ireland' and Yeats's country of the 'fanatic heart'. She once said, 'I am of Irish descent – wholly Celt.' Despite the genetic inheritance – elective to some extent – her poetic restraint is not necessarily in the Irish tradition. Pound believed her poetry to be distinctively American. He's right, of course. Spenser, author of *The Faerie Queene*, was burned out of his home, Castle Kilcolman, during the insurrection of 1598 and though there is no reference to this event in the poem certain lines have a resonance. 'The Irish say your trouble is their/trouble and your/joy their joy? I wish/I could believe it. I'm dissatisfied, I'm Irish.' Enough said!

In 'We Call Them the Brave' there are no heroics. It's not her style. 'Better not euphemize the grave.' She knows how death plays out in the 'fashionable town'. Even now, the warning resounds: what will happen 'when no one will fight for anything/and there's nothing of worth to save'?

The Mind Is an Enchanting Thing

is an enchanted thing
   like the glaze on a
katydid-wing
      subdivided by sun
      till the nettings are legion.
Like Gieseking playing Scarlatti;

like the apteryx-awl
   as a beak, or the
kiwi's rain-shawl
      of haired feathers, the mind
      feeling its way as though blind,
walks along with its eyes on the ground.

It has memory's ear
   that can hear without
having to hear.
      Like the gyroscope's fall,
      truly equivocal
because trued by regnant certainty,

it is a power of
   strong enchantment. It
is like the dove-
      neck animated by
      sun; it is memory's eye;
it's conscientious inconsistency.

It tears off the veil; tears
   the temptation, the
mist the heart wears,
      from its eyes—if the heart
      has a face; it takes apart
dejection. It's fire in the dove-neck's

iridescence; in the
   inconsistencies
of Scarlatti.
      Unconfusion submits
      its confusion to proof: it's
not a Herod's oath that cannot change.

We All Know It

That silence is best: that action and re-
Action are equal: that control, discipline, and
Liberation are bywords when spoken by an appraiser, that the
    Accidental sometimes achieves perfection, loath though we may
        be to admit it:

And that the realm of art is the realm in
Which to look for 'fishbones in the throat of the gang.' Pin-
Pricks and the unstereotyped embarrassment being the contin-
    Ual diet of artists. And in spite of it all, poets ask us just what it

Is in them that we cannot subscribe to:
People overbear till told to stop: no matter through
What sobering process they have gone, some inquire if emotion,
        true
    And stimulated are not the same thing: promoters request us to
        take our oath

That appearances are not cosmic: mis-
Fits in the world of achievement want to know what bus-
Iness people have to reserve judgment about undertakings. It is
    A strange idea that one must say what one thinks in order to be
        understood.

Silence

My father used to say,
'Superior people never make long visits,
have to be shown Longfellow's grave
or the glass flowers at Harvard.
Self-reliant like the cat—
that takes its prey to privacy,
the mouse's limp tail hanging like a shoelace from its mouth—
they sometimes enjoy solitude,
and can be robbed of speech
by speech which has delighted them.
The deepest feeling always shows itself in silence;
not in silence, but restraint.'
Nor was he insincere in saying, 'Make my house your inn.'
Inns are not residences.

To Be Liked by You Would Be a Calamity

'Attack is more piquant than concord,' but when
   You tell me frankly that you would like to feel
     My flesh beneath your feet,
       I'm all abroad; I can but put my weapon up, and
        Bow you out.
Gesticulation—it is half the language.
   Let unsheathed gesticulation be the steel
     Your courtesy must meet,
       Since in your hearing words are mute, which to my senses
        Are a shout.

Roses Only

You do not seem to realize that beauty is a liability rather than
    an asset—that in view of the fact that spirit creates form we are
        justified in supposing
            that you must have brains. For you, a symbol of the unit, stiff
                and sharp,
    conscious of surpassing by dint of native superiority and liking
        for everything
self-dependent, anything an

ambitious civilization might produce: for you, unaided, to attempt
    through sheer
    reserve to confute presumptions resulting from observation is
        idle. You cannot make us
            think you a delightful happen-so. But rose, if you are brilliant,
                it
    is not because your petals are the without-which-nothing of pre-
        eminence. You would look, minus
thorns—like a what-is-this, a mere

peculiarity. They are not proof against a storm, the elements, or
    mildew
    but what about the predatory hand? What is brilliance without
        coordination? Guarding the
        infinitesimal pieces of your mind, compelling audience to
    the remark that it is better to be forgotten than to be
        remembered too violently,
your thorns are the best part of you.

'I Like a Horse but I Have a Fellow Feeling for a Mule'

I like the mule: his sides are thin.
He takes his ease in no man's inn.
When contrarieties are thick
About his mind's eye, he will kick;
Men bewail their false position;
Closing with the mule's tradition.
He skirts the treeless precipice.
The former groan at that and this:
Though steeped in incredulity,
He treads on 'nothing' safely; he
Erects his body as a hedge
Between their bodies and the edge.

Spenser's Ireland

has not altered;—
    a place as kind as it is green,
    the greenest place I've never seen.
Every name is a tune.
Denunciations do not affect
    the culprit; nor blows, but it
is torture to him to not be spoken to.
They're natural,—
        the coat, like Venus'
mantle lined with stars,
buttoned close at the neck,—the sleeves new from disuse.

If in Ireland
    they play the harp backward at need,
    and gather at midday the seed
of the fern, eluding
their 'giants all covered with iron,' might
    there be fern seed for unlearn-
ing obduracy and for reinstating
the enchantment?
        Hindered characters
seldom have mothers
in Irish stories, but they all have grandmothers.

It was Irish;
    a match not a marriage was made
    when my great great grandmother'd said
with native genius for
disunion, 'Although your suitor be

       perfection, one objection
is enough; he is not
Irish.' Outwitting
        the fairies, befriending the furies,
whoever again
and again says, 'I'll never give in,' never sees
that you're not free
    until you've been made captive by
    supreme belief,—credulity
you say? When large dainty
fingers tremblingly divide the wings
       of the fly for mid-July
with a needle and wrap it with peacock-tail,
or the wool and
        buzzard's wing, their pride,
like the enchanter's,
is in care, not madness. Concurring hands divide

flax for damask
    that when bleached by Irish weather
    has the silvered chamois-leather
water-tightness of a
skin. Twisted torcs and gold new-moon-shaped
       lunulae aren't jewelry
like the purple-coral fuchsia-tree's. Eire—
the guillemot
       so neat and the hen
of the heath and the
linnet spinet-sweet—bespeak relentlessness? Then

they are to me
    like enchanted Earl Gerald who
    changed himself into a stag, to
a great green-eyed cat of
the mountain. Discommodity makes

them invisible; they've dis-
appeared. The Irish say your trouble is their
trouble and your
joy their joy? I wish
I could believe it. I'm dissatisfied, I'm Irish.

We Call Them the Brave

who likely were reluctant to be brave.
Sitting by a slow fire on a waste
of snow, I would last about an hour.
Better not euphemize the grave.

In this fashionable town, endearments are the mode
though generals are appraised—not praised—
and one is not forced to walk about
where a muddy slough serves as a road.

'What are these shadows barely
visible, which radar fails to scan?'
ships 'keeping distance on the gentle swell.'
And 'what is a free world ready

to do, for what it values most?'
bestow little discs the bereaved may touch?
forget it even when dead—
that congressionally honored ghost

mourned by a friend whose shoulder sags—
weeping on the shoulder of another
for another; with another sitting near,
filling out casualty tags.

What of it? We call them the brave
perhaps? Yes; what if the time should come
when no one will fight for anything
and there's nothing of worth to save.

SYLVIA PLATH

Poet and novelist, Sylvia Plath was born in Boston,
Massachusetts in 1932. *Ariel*, her famous collection
published posthumously in 1965, edited by her husband,
the poet Ted Hughes, established her iconic reputation.
She died in 1963.

SYLVIA PLATH

The Woman is Perfected

At the time of her death in 1963, aged thirty, Sylvia Plath had published just one collection of poetry, to muted response, and one novel. Yet she is now, and has been for decades, recognised as a major poet whose life and work challenge us artistically, psychologically and morally. How did this come about, this quite extraordinary posthumous fame?

The catalyst was the *Ariel* poems, discovered by her husband, the poet Ted Hughes, after her suicide in 1963, edited by him and published by Faber and Faber in 1965. Many were written in the autumn of 1962, after their separation, and the final poems in January 1963 when she was living with their two children in a flat once occupied by W. B. Yeats – a source of pleasure to her. These poems, as Erica Wagner points out in *Ariel's Gift*, were originally arranged in manuscript form by Plath begin with the word 'Love' and end with 'Spring'. Wagner also traces with poise the interconnectedness between the two poets and their poetry. Plath's last poems are a concentrated rush to greatness. And she knew it. 'When my sleeping pill wears off, I am up at about five, in my study, writing like mad.' She woke, Heaney writes, already composed in Yeats's terms into 'something intended, complete' feeling 'like a very efficient tool or weapon used and in demand from moment to moment'. She had become herself – her persona – sounding out the poems, which, as she wrote to her mother, 'will make my name my name'. They did. 'With these poems,' said Robert Lowell, she became 'something newly, wildly and subtly created, hardly a person at all or a woman but one of those super-real hypnotic great classical heroines'. Intense selfhood ('le moi profond'), as Lowell knew better than most, can be hazardous, particularly if you believe as Plath did, 'the blood jet is poetry,/There is no stopping it.' Philip Larkin said of her poems, 'They exist in a prolonged, high-pitched ecstasy, like nothing else in Literature.' He wondered, had her own talent overwhelmed her? Larkin, to whom life seemed dangerous to art, seems to pose the question: is art dangerous to life? Perhaps.

Sylvia Plath was born on 27 October 1932, in Jamaica Plain, Boston, Massachusetts, to Emil Plath, a Prussian immigrant and Professor of German at Boston University, and Aurelia Schober, a high-school teacher of Austrian extraction who was twenty years his junior. When Sylvia was eight her father, a diabetic, died as a result of surgery to remove a gangrenous leg. Everything about this death is shocking, the appalling imagery, the loss of home as well as father, the necessity for Aurelia to return to work to support her children. It left Sylvia Plath with a fierce sense of angry desolation. Childhood was over. Later, in 'Ocean 1212-W' she wrote, 'Those first nine years of my life sealed themselves off like a ship in a bottle, beautiful, obsolete, a fine, white flying myth.'

The family survived. Sylvia survived. Indeed, it would seem, she blossomed. She was a brilliant student who wrote poetry and under-stood her vocation early. She wrote, at sixteen, 'You ask me why I spend my life writing/do I find entertainment?/Is it worthwhile?/ Above all does it pay? I write only because there is a voice within me which will not be stilled.' She eventually attended Smith College supported by a scholarship. She was a social success, extremely pretty and popular; was on the board of the college; was shortlisted for poetry prizes; and was guest editor for the fashion magazine *Mademoiselle*. On the surface, a *jeunesse dorée*. This surface impression of intelligent, attractive gaiety was to last well into her twenties. 'What was she like?' Eileen Atkins asked Charles Osborne, after a poetry reading I'd organised years ago. 'Well,' said Charles, who knew Sylvia Plath during her years in London, 'initially, she struck me as a very pretty, very vivacious American cheerleader.' That same evening a man came up to me and said, 'This is the first time I've ever been frightened by poetry.'

From her teenage years onwards Sylvia Plath suffered from severe depression and Aurelia, aware that the illness was endemic in Otto's family, sought help, including electroconvulsive treatment. In 1953 when she was twenty-one she attempted suicide and began the intensive therapy that she would continue throughout her short life. Considerable strength of character was required for her to hold hard to her dreams of academic excellence and artistic fulfilment, and to return to Smith. Her brilliance and her perseverance won her a Fulbright Scholarship to study at Newnham College, Cambridge, and in the autumn of 1955 she set sail for England.

Nine months later, after a serious *coup de foudre*, Sylvia Plath, aged twenty-three, married the poet Ted Hughes, aged twenty-five, on 16 June 1956, Bloomsday for Joyce fans. Of her first meeting with him she wrote to her mother, 'I shall tell you something most miraculous and thundering and terrifying. It is this man I have never known anything like it ... The more he writes poems the more he writes poems ... daily I too am full of poems ... my joy whirls in tongues of words ... I shall be a woman beyond women.' These are the words of an ecstatic, and ecstatics are born, not made. 'Marriage, Iris Murdoch believed, 'is a very private place.' Because of its tragic aftermath few marriages have been subjected to more analysis than that of the young poets Sylvia Plath and Ted Hughes. Possibly because their story weaves together art and passion with the intensity of Greek tragedy, Janet Malcolm, Diane Middlebrook, Jacqueline Rose, Anne Stevenson and Erica Wagner are among the many who with honour have approached this modern tale of abiding sadness. At the end of his life, having not 'spoken' before (the protection of children often demands silence), Ted Hughes wrote the haunting *Birthday Letters*.

Suffice to say here that their seven years together were drenched in passion and pain, as the two hugely ambitious, mutually supportive poets set up home, had children – Frieda in 1960, Nicholas in January 1962 – all the while trying to make a living and striving daily, hourly, endlessly, to create great poetry. It was a full life, perhaps overwhelmingly so. Her early poetry did not come easily to Plath, who during their marriage, Ted Hughes said, 'composed very slowly, consulting her Thesaurus and dictionary for almost every word, putting a slow strong line of ink under each word that attracted her'. She herself once said she'd rather live with her thesaurus than a bible on a desert island. She had a 'vision' of the kind of poems she would like to write but '[I] do not. When will they come?' They were waiting. The marriage, already under strain, was broken by Ted Hughes' affair with Assia Wevill and they separated in August 1962. In the autumn of the same year Plath wrote most of the poems that made her immortal.

On 10 February 1963, having had flu, as had her children, during one of the coldest Januarys on record, Sylvia Plath took her own life. Her mother wrote, 'Her physical energies having been depleted by illness, anxiety and overwork and although she had for so long managed to be gallant and equal to the life experience, some darker day than usual had temporarily made it seem impossible to pursue'. Seamus Heaney took, as the title of his essay on Plath, a line from one of her last poems, 'The indefatigable hoof-taps'. They continue to reverberate.

The Poems

'Because I could not stop for Death –/He kindly stopped for me,' wrote Emily Dickinson. Well, Plath stopped for him. And as an artist, at a most particular moment – one of secret fulfilment. Even in an early Plath poem, 'Mushrooms', one can hear an underground note of advancement – determined, almost military, as the usually benign mushroom warns us, 'Our foot's in the door.' Plath's feeling for syllable and rhythm, which Eliot marked as one of the key components in the auditory imagination, is already apparent.

'The Colossus' is her father, writ large. 'Thirty years now I have labored/To dredge the silt from your throat./I am none the wiser.' It's an old story. 'The Colossus' was the title poem of her first collection, which itself went through endless permutations, including, as Hughes points out, the telling *Full Fathom Five*, also, and just as compelling and provocative, *The Bull of Bendylaw*.

Philip Larkin wrote of the opening lines of 'Two Views of a Cadaver Room', 'the shock is sudden'. He'd read the poems chronologically and, though impressed, this is the poem of which he said, 'The possibility that she is simply trying on another style is dispelled' and, he continues, 'she has found her subject matter'. It is a line that tolls like a bell. The painting referred to in the poem is Pieter Bruegel's *Triumph of Death* and there are echoes also, I believe, of the poet Gottfried Benn's *Morgue*.

Plath died young and virtually unknown. So I quote her where possible on her own work. Of the speaker in 'The Applicant', she said, He 'is an executive . . . [who] wants to be sure the applicant for his marvelous product . . . will treat it right.' The question, 'Will you marry it, marry it, marry it' strikes a sinister, Pinteresque note. She was much criticised for her almost obsessive use of repetition, as Tim Kendall points out in *Sylvia Plath: A Critical Study*. However, in her inner ear that is how Plath heard the beat. Like Lear's 'never', repeated five times, to sound his despair at Cordelia's death, the human voice releases the power of repetition from the page. Of 'Death & Co.' she said, it 'is about the double or schizophrenic nature of death – the marmoreal coldness of Blake's death mask, say, hand in glove with the fearful softness of worms . . . I imagine these two aspects of death as two men . . . who have come to call.' There is nothing to add.

The wild rhythms and the terrifying energy of 'Daddy', are controlled, just, by the artist. She herself said of it, 'Here is a poem spoken by a girl with an Electra complex. Her father died while she thought he was God.' Camille Paglia described it as 'garish, sarcastic and profane and one of the strongest poems ever written by a woman'. It would take a strong woman to disagree.

At a BBC reading (and few writers loved the BBC more than Plath), she introduced the dramatic monologue of 'Lady Lazarus' thus: 'The speaker is a woman who has the great and terrible gift of being reborn. The only trouble is, she has to die first.' The lines 'I rise with my red hair/And I eat men like air' are terrifying. In 'Edge', 'The woman is perfected'.

Mushrooms

Overnight, very
Whitely, discreetly,
Very quietly

Our toes, our noses
Take hold on the loam,
Acquire the air.

Nobody sees us,
Stops us, betrays us;
The small grains make room.

Soft fists insist on
Heaving the needles,
The leafy bedding,

Even the paving.
Our hammers, our rams,
Earless and eyeless,

Perfectly voiceless,
Widen the crannies,
Shoulder through holes. We

Diet on water,
On crumbs of shadow,
Bland-mannered, asking

Little or nothing.
So many of us!
So many of us!

We are shelves, we are
Tables, we are meek,
We are edible,

Nudgers and shovers
In spite of ourselves.
Our kind multiplies:

We shall by morning
Inherit the earth.
Our foot's in the door.

The Colossus

I shall never get you put together entirely,
Pieced, glued, and properly jointed.
Mule-bray, pig-grunt and bawdy cackles
Proceed from your great lips.
It's worse than a barnyard.

Perhaps you consider yourself an oracle,
Mouthpiece of the dead, or of some god or other.
Thirty years now I have labored
To dredge the silt from your throat.
I am none the wiser.

Scaling little ladders with gluepots and pails of Lysol
I crawl like an ant in mourning
Over the weedy acres of your brow
To mend the immense skull-plates and clear
The bald, white tumuli of your eyes.

A blue sky out of the Oresteia
Arches above us. O father, all by yourself
You are pithy and historical as the Roman Forum.
I open my lunch on a hill of black cypress.
Your fluted bones and acanthine hair are littered

In their old anarchy to the horizon-line.
It would take more than a lightning-stroke
To create such a ruin.
Nights, I squat in the cornucopia
Of your left ear, out of the wind,

Counting the red stars and those of plum-color.
The sun rises under the pillar of your tongue.
My hours are married to shadow.
No longer do I listen for the scrape of a keel
On the blank stones of the landing.

Two Views of a Cadaver Room

(1)

The day she visited the dissecting room
They had four men laid out, black as burnt turkey,
Already half unstrung. A vinegary fume
Of the death vats clung to them;
The white-smocked boys started working.
The head of his cadaver had caved in,
And she could scarcely make out anything
In that rubble of skull plates and old leather.
A sallow piece of string held it together.

In their jars the snail-nosed babies moon and glow.
He hands her the cut-out heart like a cracked heirloom.

(2)

In Brueghel's panorama of smoke and slaughter
Two people only are blind to the carrion army:
He, afloat in the sea of her blue satin
Skirts, sings in the direction
Of her bare shoulder, while she bends,
Fingering a leaflet of music, over him,
Both of them deaf to the fiddle in the hands
Of the death's-head shadowing their song.
These Flemish lovers flourish; not for long.

Yet desolation, stalled in paint, spares the little country
Foolish, delicate, in the lower right hand corner.

The Applicant

First, are you our sort of a person?
Do you wear
A glass eye, false teeth or a crutch,
A brace or a hook,
Rubber breasts or a rubber crotch,

Stitches to show something's missing? No, no? Then
How can we give you a thing?
Stop crying.
Open your hand.
Empty? Empty. Here is a hand

To fill it and willing
To bring teacups and roll away headaches
And do whatever you tell it.
Will you marry it?
It is guaranteed

To thumb shut your eyes at the end
And dissolve of sorrow.
We make new stock from the salt.
I notice you are stark naked.
How about this suit—

Black and stiff, but not a bad fit.
Will you marry it?
It is waterproof, shatterproof, proof
Against fire and bombs through the roof.
Believe me, they'll bury you in it.

Now your head, excuse me, is empty.
I have the ticket for that.
Come here, sweetie, out of the closet.
Well, what do you think of *that*?
Naked as paper to start

But in twenty-five years she'll be silver,
In fifty, gold.
A living doll, everywhere you look.
It can sew, it can cook,
It can talk, talk, talk.

It works, there is nothing wrong with it.
You have a hole, it's a poultice.
You have an eye, it's an image.
My boy, it's your last resort.
Will you marry it, marry it, marry it.

Death & Co.

Two, of course there are two.
It seems perfectly natural now—
The one who never looks up, whose eyes are lidded
And balled, like Blake's,
Who exhibits

The birthmarks that are his trademark—
The scald scar of water,
The nude
Verdigris of the condor.
I am red meat. His beak

Claps sidewise: I am not his yet.
He tells me how badly I photograph.
He tells me how sweet
The babies look in their hospital
Icebox, a simple

Frill at the neck,
Then the flutings of their Ionian
Death-gowns,
Then two little feet.
He does not smile or smoke.

The other does that,
His hair long and plausive.
Bastard
Masturbating a glitter,
He wants to be loved.

I do not stir.
The frost makes a flower,
The dew makes a star,
The dead bell,
The dead bell.

Somebody's done for.

Daddy

You do not do, you do not do
Any more, black shoe
In which I have lived like a foot
For thirty years, poor and white,
Barely daring to breathe or Achoo.

Daddy, I have had to kill you.
You died before I had time—
Marble-heavy, a bag full of God,
Ghastly statue with one gray toe
Big as a Frisco seal

And a head in the freakish Atlantic
Where it pours bean green over blue
In the waters off beautiful Nauset.
I used to pray to recover you.
Ach, du.

In the German tongue, in the Polish town
Scraped flat by the roller
Of wars, wars, wars.
But the name of the town is common.
My Polack friend

Says there are a dozen or two.
So I never could tell where you
Put your foot, your root,
I never could talk to you.

The tongue stuck in my jaw.

It stuck in a barb wire snare.
Ich, ich, ich, ich,
I could hardly speak.
I thought every German was you.
And the language obscene

An engine, an engine
Chuffing me off like a Jew.
A Jew to Dachau, Auschwitz, Belsen.
I began to talk like a Jew.
I think I may well be a Jew.

The snows of the Tyrol, the clear beer of Vienna
Are not very pure or true.
With my gypsy ancestress and my weird luck
And my Taroc pack and my Taroc pack
I may be a bit of a Jew.

I have always been scared of *you*,
With your Luftwaffe, your gobbledygoo.
And your neat mustache
And your Aryan eye, bright blue.
Panzer-man, panzer-man, O You—

Not God but a swastika
So black no sky could squeak through.
Every woman adores a Fascist,
The boot in the face, the brute
Brute heart of a brute like you.

You stand at the blackboard, daddy,
In the picture I have of you,
A cleft in your chin instead of your foot

But no less a devil for that, no not
Any less the black man who

Bit my pretty red heart in two.
I was ten when they buried you.
At twenty I tried to die
And get back, back, back to you.
I thought even the bones would do.

But they pulled me out of the sack,
And they stuck me together with glue.
And then I knew what to do.
I made a model of you,
A man in black with a Meinkampf look

And a love of the rack and the screw.
And I said I do, I do.
So daddy, I'm finally through.
The black telephone's off at the root,
The voices just can't worm through.

If I've killed one man, I've killed two—
The vampire who said he was you
And drank my blood for a year,
Seven years, if you want to know.
Daddy, you can lie back now.

There's a stake in your fat black heart
And the villagers never liked you.
They are dancing and stamping on you.
They always *knew* it was you.
Daddy, daddy, you bastard, I'm through.

Lady Lazarus

I have done it again.
One year in every ten
I manage it—

A sort of walking miracle, my skin
Bright as a Nazi lampshade,
My right foot

A paperweight,
My face a featureless, fine
Jew linen.

Peel off the napkin
O my enemy,
Do I terrify?—

The nose, the eye pits, the full set of teeth?
The sour breath
Will vanish in a day.

Soon, soon the flesh
The grave cave ate will be
At home on me

And I a smiling woman.
I am only thirty.
And like the cat I have nine times to die.

This is Number Three.
What a trash
To annihilate each decade.

What a million filaments.
The peanut-crunching crowd
Shoves in to see

Them unwrap me hand and foot—
The big strip tease.
Gentlemen, ladies

These are my hands
My knees.
I may be skin and bone,

Nevertheless, I am the same, identical woman.
The first time it happened I was ten.
It was an accident.

The second time I meant
To last it out and not come back at all.
I rocked shut

As a seashell.
They had to call and call
And pick the worms off me like sticky pearls.

Dying
Is an art, like everything else.
I do it exceptionally well.

I do it so it feels like hell.
I do it so it feels real.
I guess you could say I've a call.

It's easy enough to do it in a cell.
It's easy enough to do it and stay put.
It's the theatrical

Comeback in broad day
To the same place, the same face, the same brute
Amused shout:

'A miracle!'
That knocks me out.
There is a charge

For the eyeing of my scars, there is a charge
For the hearing of my heart—
It really goes.

And there is a charge, a very large charge
For a word or a touch
Or a bit of blood

Or a piece of my hair or my clothes.
So, so, Herr Doktor.
So, Herr Enemy.

I am your opus,
I am your valuable,
The pure gold baby

That melts to a shriek.
I turn and burn.
Do not think I underestimate your great concern.

Ash, ash—
You poke and stir.
Flesh, bone, there is nothing there—

A cake of soap,
A wedding ring,
A gold filling.

Herr God, Herr Lucifer
Beware
Beware.

Out of the ash
I rise with my red hair
And I eat men like air.

Edge

The woman is perfected.
Her dead

Body wears the smile of accomplishment,
The illusion of a Greek necessity

Flows in the scrolls of her toga,
Her bare

Feet seem to be saying:
We have come so far, it is over.

Each dead child coiled, a white serpent,
One at each little

Pitcher of milk, now empty.
She has folded

Them back into her body as petals
Of a rose close when the garden

Stiffens and odors bleed
From the sweet, deep throats of the night flower.

The moon has nothing to be sad about,
Staring from her hood of bone.

She is used to this sort of thing.
Her blacks crackle and drag.

WILLIAM BUTLER YEATS

William Butler Yeats was born in Dublin in 1865. Poet,
playwright and critic, he was a founder member of The
Abbey Theatre in his native city. *The Wanderings of Oisin*
(1889) immediately established his reputation. He won the
Nobel Prize in 1923 and died in 1939.

WILLIAM BUTLER YEATS

A Pity Beyond All Telling

'If a powerful and benevolent spirit has shaped the destiny of this world we can better discover that destiny from the words that have gathered up the heart's desire of the world.' Yeats found them in English, in Ireland. The publication in 1889 of William Butler Yeats's first book of poetry, *The Wanderings of Oisin*, was a seminal moment, not only in Irish literature but in Irish political history. The Gaelic League, started in 1893 by Douglas Hyde, had as its express purpose the continuation of the Celtic tradition in the language of Gaelic. Yeats, whose first book was based on the ancient Fenian cycle, would from then on bring Irish mythology to the Irish people in the English language: the language in which, Yeats pointed out, 'modern Ireland thinks and does its business.

Roy Foster's essential, magisterial, two-part biography of Yeats, *The Apprentice Mage* and *The Arch-Poet*, weaves from poetry, personality and history a tale of creation – not only of a poet but of a literature and a society. Yeats was born in 1865 (his brother Jack is the celebrated painter) to John Butler Yeats, the son of rectors in the Church of Ireland, and to Susan Pollexfen, whose shipbuilding family came from Sligo. It was she who filled his head with the strange visions and the folklore of the area – which is perhaps why Joyce said of him, 'He had a surrealist imagination few painters could match.' As Foster shows us, Yeats learned early that art is what matters. His father, a solicitor, gave up his practice to study painting in London. Yeats went, not very happily, to Godolphin School (now Godolphin and

Latymer) in Hammersmith, where, bizarrely, he became the best high diver in the school. He returned to Dublin, studied art and finally, in one of literature's luckiest volte-face, decided on poetry. In Yeats, as Foster tells us, all the great gifts combine: 'the feeling for syllable and rhythm' that is essential to what Eliot called 'the auditory imagination', the visual sensibility of the trained painter; and the alchemist's power to transform language, so that it steals us away, with other-world words, to the 'Land of Heart's Desire'.

In Irish literature Yeats resembles a tidal wave. The tide was not only poetical. In 1904, Yeats set up the National Theatre of Ireland, the Abbey Theatre, with Lady Gregory. In his Nobel speech to the Swedish Academy in 1923, he chose as his subject, not poetry, but the Irish dramatic movement. 'I would not be here were I not the symbol of that movement. When we thought of the plays we would like to perform we thought of what was romantic and poetical, for the nationalism we had called up – like that every generation had called up in moments of discouragement – was romantic and poetical.'

Well, up to a point. Yeats, the artist who claimed the 'romantic and poetical' for Irish nationalism, also, with his genius for spotting genius in others, brought to the Abbey Theatre Synge's *The Playboy of the Western World* and O'Casey's *The Plough and the Stars*. The Abbey audience was possibly the most hypersensitive in history. The plays were provocative. They rioted, frequently. Yeats fought back. He harangued them from the stage – 'You have disgraced yourselves, again' – and he persevered. This strength of character and courage in the face of prejudice, which was noted by Eliot, is fundamental to his astonishing achievements. As a senator he was to endeavour to get a 'bill of divorcement' through the Irish Senate. He failed. The fact that he tried at all is astonishing. Finally, he refused to allow himself to be destroyed by the agony of his unreciprocated, lifelong obsession with Maude Gonne, an obsession that would have felled lesser men.

She exploded into his life in 1889 just after the publication of *The Wanderings of Oisin*. Foster charts her tempestuous journey through the life of the poet. She was young, twenty-two, tall, with 'flaming' hair, but it was her passion that 'began all the trouble of my life'. She took possession of his soul – when the soul is lost to a woman, all is lost – and she inspired some of the greatest love poetry ever written. He had found the love of his life; she had found a poet for the cause. She was magnificent, brave and dangerous, with a fanatical love of Ireland – although not Irish herself – and was twice imprisoned for her activities. She described the British Empire as 'the outward symbol of Satan in the world'. Understatement was not her thing. Yeats wrote of her, 'She lived in storm and strife,/Her soul had such desire/For what proud death may bring/That it could not endure/ The common good of life,'. And therein lies the pity. Her fanaticism swept away much that was good in her life. His enduring love, expressed in poems of genius, gave us the strange poetry of the exultant, broken heart.

She married Sean MacBride, a revolutionary as extreme as she – Foster tells us they spent part of their honeymoon 'allegedly reconnoitering assassination attempts for an impending Royal visit to Gibraltar'. The confirmation of their marriage was, Yeats said, 'like lightning through me'. Their union was a disaster and they separated after five years. Sean MacBride was executed with the leaders of the 1916 rebellion.

In his fifties Yeats married Georgie Hyde-Lees, with whom he had two adored children, Anne and Michael. He was 'capable of experience' and, in embracing life with passion and courage in both the private and the public spheres, he did what no poet has ever done before or since: he wrote some of his greatest work in his sixties and seventies. 'Maturing as a poet,' Eliot wrote, means 'maturing as a whole man . . . out of his [Yeats's] intense experience he now expressed universal truths. An artist by serving his art with his entire integrity, is at the same time rendering the greatest service he can to his country and to the whole world.' Ireland owes him.

William Butler Yeats is buried in the Sligo he loved, beneath 'bare Ben Bulben's head'. His epitaph reads, as he requested: 'Cast a cold eye/On life, on death./Horseman, pass by.'

The Poems

'The Pity of Love' has one of the loveliest lines in poetry: 'A pity beyond all telling/Is hid in the heart of love:' More provocatively, in 'The Tower' Yeats posed another question about love: 'Does the imagination dwell the most/Upon a woman won or woman lost?' In 'The Folly of Being Comforted' it seems that either way, there 'ain't no cure for love'. It survives the loss of beauty, youth, vitality – and rages on. 'O heart! O heart! If she'd but turn her head,/You'd know the folly of being comforted.'

In 'Friends' the gentle beauty of Olivia Shakespeare, with whom he had an affair after falling in love with Maud Gonne (to follow Maud Gonne meant one was always second), is praised, as is the indomitable spirit of Lady Gregory. And the third friend in this famous poem, what of Maude Gonne? Twenty-three years after he'd met her he writes that when he thinks of her 'up from my heart's root/So great a sweetness flows/I shake from head to foot.' Long, long love. 'Women, Beware Women', wrote Thomas Middleton. What do they want? The utterly impossible, as Freud probably knew. In 'Before the World was made' the narrator searches in mirror after mirror for her mythical, mystical face. She is not in quest of a Lacan-like moment of psychological insight but of the power that would entice her lover to 'love the thing that was/Before the world was made.' It's a little-known poem and undeservedly so.

The poem 'Easter, 1916' was inspired by the tragic military failure of the rebellion, of which Yeats wrote to Lady Gregory: 'I had no idea that any public event could so deeply move me . . . all the work of years has been overturned.' The patriotic self-sacrifice of MacDonagh and MacBride, Connolly and Pearse, led to the poem that presages the birth of a nation. The iconic line 'A terrible beauty is born' contains both warning and blessing. The word 'terrible', I believe, requires equal weight with the word 'beauty'. The rhythms and repetitions in the poem seem to keep pace almost irresistibly with the destiny of the men. The lines 'Too long a sacrifice/Can make a stone of the heart,' sound another note of ambivalence, which was possibly the reason that Maud Gonne was less than impressed by the poem.

'The Municipal Gallery Re-visited' is, he said, 'a poem about the Ireland we have all served, and the movement of which I have been a part'. He had just visited the gallery and, as he looked at the portraits of so many old friends, memories of old loves flooded in: 'Think where man's glory most begins and ends/And say my glory was I had such friends.'

'Adam's Curse' reminds us, as he once wrote, that 'we achieve, if we do achieve, in little sedentary stitches as though we were making lace'. Often in secret, 'All that is beautiful in art is laboured over' in 'the hidden hours unnoticed by bankers, schoolmasters and clergymen'. 'Yet if it does not seem a moment's thought,/Our stitching and unstitching has been naught.' And love? 'We sat grown quiet at the name of love . . . I had a thought . . . That you were beautiful, and that I strove/To love you in the old high way of love.'

'The Circus Animals' Desertion', written late in life, is one of the greatest poems ever to deal with the creative tension between art and life. Yeats says, 'Maybe at last being but a broken man/I must be satisfied with my heart', and continues: 'Now that my ladder's gone/I must lie down where all the ladders start/In the foul rag and bone shop of the heart.' Where else?

The Pity of Love

A pity beyond all telling
Is hid in the heart of love:
The folk who are buying and selling,
The clouds on their journey above,
The cold wet winds ever blowing,
And the shadowy hazel grove
Where mouse-grey waters are flowing,
Threaten the head that I love.

The Folly of Being Comforted

One that is ever kind said yesterday:
'Your well-belovèd's hair has threads of grey,
And little shadows come about her eyes;
Time can but make it easier to be wise
Though now it seems impossible, and so
All that you need is patience.'
                                Heart cries, 'No,
I have not a crumb of comfort, not a grain.
Time can but make her beauty over again:
Because of that great nobleness of hers
The fire that stirs about her, when she stirs,
Burns but more clearly. O she had not these ways
When all the wild summer was in her gaze.'

O heart! O heart! if she'd but turn her head,
You'd know the folly of being comforted.

Friends

Now must I these three praise –
Three women that have wrought
What joy is in my days:
One because no thought,
Nor those unpassing cares,
No, not in these fifteen
Many-times-troubled years,
Could ever come between
Mind and delighted mind;
And one because her hand
Had strength that could unbind
What none can understand,
What none can have and thrive,
Youth's dreamy load, till she
So changed me that I live
Labouring in ecstasy.
And what of her that took
All till my youth was gone
With scarce a pitying look?
How could I praise that one?
When day begins to break
I count my good and bad,
Being wakeful for her sake,
Remembering what she had,
What eagle look still shows,
While up from my heart's root
So great a sweetness flows
I shake from head to foot.

Before the World was made

If I make the lashes dark
And the eyes more bright
And the lips more scarlet,
Or ask if all be right
From mirror after mirror,
No vanity's displayed:
I'm looking for the face I had
Before the world was made.

What if I look upon a man
As though on my beloved,
And my blood be cold the while
And my heart unmoved?
Why should he think me cruel
Or that he is betrayed?
I'd have him love the thing that was
Before the world was made.

Easter, 1916

I have met them at close of day
Coming with vivid faces
From counter or desk among grey
Eighteenth-century houses.
I have passed with a nod of the head
Or polite meaningless words,
Or have lingered awhile and said
Polite meaningless words,
And thought before I had done
Of a mocking tale or a gibe
To please a companion
Around the fire at the club,
Being certain that they and I
But lived where motley is worn:
All changed, changed utterly:
A terrible beauty is born.

That woman's days were spent
In ignorant good-will,
Her nights in argument
Until her voice grew shrill.
What voice more sweet than hers
When, young and beautiful,
She rode to harriers?
This man had kept a school
And rode our wingèd horse;
This other his helper and friend
Was coming into his force;

He might have won fame in the end,
So sensitive his nature seemed,
So daring and sweet his thought.
This other man I had dreamed
A drunken, vainglorious lout.
He had done most bitter wrong
To some who are near my heart,
Yet I number him in the song;
He, too, has resigned his part
In the casual comedy;
He, too, has been changed in his turn,
Transformed utterly:
A terrible beauty is born.

Hearts with one purpose alone
Through summer and winter seem
Enchanted to a stone
To trouble the living stream.
The horse that comes from the road,
The rider, the birds that range
From cloud to tumbling cloud,
Minute by minute they change;
A shadow of cloud on the stream
Changes minute by minute;
A horse-hoof slides on the brim,
And a horse plashes within it;
The long-legged moor-hens dive,
And hens to moor-cocks call;
Minute by minute they live:
The stone's in the midst of all.

Too long a sacrifice
Can make a stone of the heart.
O when may it suffice?
That is Heaven's part, our part

To murmur name upon name,
As a mother names her child
When sleep at last has come
On limbs that had run wild.
What is it but nightfall?
No, no, not night but death;
Was it needless death after all?
For England may keep faith
For all that is done and said.
We know their dream; enough
To know they dreamed and are dead;
And what if excess of love
Bewildered them till they died?
I write it out in a verse—
MacDonagh and MacBride
And Connolly and Pearse
Now and in time to be,
Wherever green is worn,
Are changed, changed utterly:
A terrible beauty is born.

The Municipal Gallery Re-visited

I
Around me the images of thirty years;
An ambush; pilgrims at the water-side;
Casement upon trial, half hidden by the bars,
Guarded; Griffith staring in hysterical pride;
Kevin O'Higgins' countenance that wears
A gentle questioning look that cannot hide
A soul incapable of remorse or rest;
A revolutionary soldier kneeling to be blessed.

II
An Abbot or Archbishop with an upraised hand
Blessing the Tricolour. 'This is not,' I say,
'The dead Ireland of my youth, but an Ireland
The poets have imagined, terrible and gay.'
Before a woman's portrait suddenly I stand;
Beautiful and gentle in her Venetian way.
I met her all but fifty years ago
For twenty minutes in some studio.

III
Heart smitten with emotion I sink down,
My heart recovering with covered eyes;
Wherever I had looked I had looked upon
My permanent or impermanent images;
Augusta Gregory's son; her sister's son,
Hugh Lane, 'onlie begetter' of all these;

Hazel Lavery living and dying, that tale
As though some ballad singer had sung it all.

IV

Mancini's portrait of Augusta Gregory,
'Greatest since Rembrandt,' according to John Synge;
A great ebullient portrait certainly;
But where is the brush that could show anything
Of all that pride and that humility,
And I am in despair that time may bring
Approved patterns of women or of men
But not that selfsame excellence again.

V

My mediaeval knees lack health until they bend,
But in that woman, in that household where
Honour had lived so long, all lacking found.
Childless I thought, 'My children may find here
Deep-rooted things,' but never foresaw its end,
And now that end has come I have not wept;
No fox can foul the lair the badger swept.

VI

(An image out of Spenser and the common tongue.)
John Synge, I and Augusta Gregory, thought
All that we did, all that we said or sang
Must come from contact with the soil, from that
Contact everything Antaeus-like grew strong.
We three alone in modern times had brought
Everything down to that sole test again,
Dream of the noble and the beggarman.

VII

And here's John Synge himself, that rooted man
'Forgetting human words,' a grave deep face.

You that would judge me do not judge alone
This book or that, come to this hallowed place
Where my friends' portraits hang and look thereon;
Ireland's history in their lineaments trace;
Think where man's glory most begins and ends
And say my glory was I had such friends.

Adam's Curse

We sat together at one summer's end,
That beautiful mild woman, your close friend,
And you and I, and talked of poetry.
I said, 'A line will take us hours maybe;
Yet if it does not seem a moment's thought,
Our stitching and unstitching has been naught.
Better go down upon your marrow-bones
And scrub a kitchen pavement, or break stones
Like an old pauper, in all kinds of weather;
For to articulate sweet sounds together
Is to work harder than all these, and yet
Be thought an idler by the noisy set
Of bankers, schoolmasters, and clergymen
The martyrs call the world.'

                         And thereupon
That beautiful mild woman for whose sake
There's many a one shall find out all heartache
On finding that her voice is sweet and low
Replied, 'To be born woman is to know –
Although they do not talk of it at school –
That we must labour to be beautiful.'

I said, 'It's certain there is no fine thing
Since Adam's fall but needs much labouring.
There have been lovers who thought love should be
So much compounded of high courtesy
That they would sigh and quote with learned looks

Precedents out of beautiful old books;
Yet now it seems an idle trade enough.'

We sat grown quiet at the name of love;
We saw the last embers of daylight die,
And in the trembling blue-green of the sky
A moon, worn as if it had been a shell
Washed by time's waters as they rose and fell
About the stars and broke in days and years.

I had a thought for no one's but your ears:
That you were beautiful, and that I strove
To love you in the old high way of love;
That it had all seemed happy, and yet we'd grown
As weary-hearted as that hollow moon.

The Circus Animals' Desertion

I

I sought a theme and sought for it in vain,
I sought it daily for six weeks or so.
Maybe at last being but a broken man
I must be satisfied with my heart, although
Winter and summer till old age began
My circus animals were all on show,
Those stilted boys, that burnished chariot,
Lion and woman and the Lord knows what.

II

What can I but enumerate old themes,
First that sea-rider Oisin led by the nose
Through three enchanted islands, allegorical dreams,
Vain gaiety, vain battle, vain repose,
Themes of the embittered heart, or so it seems,
That might adorn old songs or courtly shows;
But what cared I that set him on to ride,
I, starved for the bosom of his fairy bride.

And then a counter-truth filled out its play,
The Countess Cathleen was the name I gave it,
She, pity-crazed, had given her soul away
But masterful Heaven had intervened to save it.
I thought my dear must her own soul destroy
So did fanaticism and hate enslave it,
And this brought forth a dream and soon enough
This dream itself had all my thought and love.

And when the Fool and Blind Man stole the bread
Cuchulain fought the ungovernable sea;
Heart mysteries there, and yet when all is said
It was the dream itself enchanted me:
Character isolated by a deed
To engross the present and dominate memory.
Players and painted stage took all my love
And not those things that they were emblems of.

III
Those masterful images because complete
Grew in pure mind but out of what began?
A mound of refuse or the sweepings of a street,
Old kettles, old bottles, and a broken can,
Old iron, old bones, old rags, that raving slut
Who keeps the till. Now that my ladder's gone
I must lie down where all the ladders start
In the foul rag and bone shop of the heart.

ACTORS' NOTES

A selection of the poems in this book are read by the following on the attached CD.

Sinéad Cusack joined the Royal Shakespeare Company in 1979 from her native Dublin. She won the coveted Clarence Derwent Award for Best Newcomer for her lead performances in *The Taming of The Shrew*, *The Merchant of Venice* and *Much Ado About Nothing*. Further acclaim followed on the London stage. Her stunning portrayal of Mai O'Hara in Sebastian Barry's *Our Lady of Sligo* at the Royal National Theatre won the *Evening Standard* Award and the Critics' Drama Award for Best Actress in 1998. She starred in Tom Stoppard's *Rock 'n' Roll*, which transferred from The Royal Court Theatre to The Duke of York. Her many film credits include Bertolucci's *Stealing Beauty* and Zeffirelli's *The Sparrow*.

Ralph Fiennes joined the Royal National Theatre in 1987 straight from RADA. In 1993 his performance in Steven Spielberg's film *Schindler's List* earned him Academy Award and Golden Globe nominations and won the BAFTA Award for Best Supporting Actor. His work in *Quiz Show*, *The English Patient*, *The End of the Affair* and *The Constant Gardener* led to further nominations including Academy Award, BAFTA and Golden Globe. A great classical actor, his legendary Hamlet, directed by Jonathan Kent, won the Tony Award for Best Actor in 1996. In 2006 his performance in Brian Friel's *The Faith Healer* was again nominated for a Tony Award. Ralph Fiennes is a UNICEF Ambassador.

Edward Fox, a graduate of RADA, has won four coveted BAFTA awards. His Most Promising Newcomer was followed by Best

Supporting Actor Awards in *The Go-Between* in 1972, *A Bridge Too Far* in 1978, *Edward and Mrs Simpson* in 1979, and in 1983 he was again nominated for *Gandhi*. His chilling lead performance in *Day of the Jackal* brought worldwide fame. A consummate theatre actor he starred in the legendary 1968 production of T.S. Eliot's *The Cocktail Party* and garnered further acclaim in Simon Gray's *Quartermaine's Terms in 1981*, *The Old Masters* in 2005 and in Shaw's *You Never Can Tell* in 2006. Edward Fox was awarded an OBE in 2003 for his services to film and theatre.

Bob Geldof was born in Ireland and in 1975 became lead singer of the highly successful The Boomtown Rats. He continues to write and perform music. He is the co-founder of several television production and technological companies. In 1984, shocked by television pictures of famine in Ethiopia, he created Band Aid, followed by Live Aid and Live 8. He has raised unprecedented sums to eradicate poverty and disease, and through his unceasing global political activism has brought to world attention the underlying causes of Third World deprivation. Bob Geldof was awarded an honorary knighthood from the Queen in 1986, and has been nominated for the Nobel Peace Prize. In 2006 he was made a Free Man of the City of Dublin.

Helen McCrory began her career at the National Theatre and the Royal Shakespeare Company. She won the Shakespeare Globe Most Promising Newcomer Award. In 2002 she was nominated for the *Evening Standard* Best Actress Award for her dual roles in *Uncle Vanya* and *Twelfth Night* at the Donmar Warehouse. In 2006 her portrayal of Rosalind in *As You Like It* won a Laurence Olivier Best Actress Award nomination. Her television awards include the Royal Television Society Best Actress Award and the Critics' Circle Best Actress Award. Her film credits include *Charlotte Grey*, *Enduring Love*, *Casanova* and *The Queen* for Stephen Frears.

Ian McDiarmid studied at the Royal Academy, Glasgow, and won the prestigious Gold Medal. His many leading stage roles include *The*

Black Prince, *Volpone*, *The Jew of Malta* and Prospero in *The Tempest*. In 2005, he played the title roles in Edward Bond's *Lear* and Tom Stoppard's new version of Pirandello's *Henry IV*. As joint Artistic Director of London's Almeida Theatre with Jonathan Kent he was awarded the coveted *Evening Standard* Award for Outstanding Contribution to Theatre. On Broadway in 2006, he won a Tony Award for his performance as Teddy in Brian Friel's *Faith Healer*. His chilling Emperor Palpatine in George Lucas's *Star Wars* series has brought him worldwide recognition.

Elizabeth McGovern made her film debut in Robert Redford's Oscar-winning *Ordinary People* and the following year she earned an Academy Award nomination as Best Supporting Actress for her performance in *Ragtime*. She garnered further acclaim in *The House of Mirth*, *The Wings of the Dove* and *The Truth*. A noted classical actress, her work in theatre includes *A Midsummer Night's Dream*, *The Three Sisters*, *Hamlet* and *The Misanthrope*. Her many television performances include *Tales from the Crypt*, *New Hampshire* and her astonishing portrayal of Beatrice-Joanna opposite Bob Hoskins in the Jacobean tragedy *The Changeling*.

Roger Moore was cast as James Bond in *Live and Let Die* in 1973, having previously starred as Simon Templar in *The Saint* - one of the longest-running series in British television history - and *The Persuaders* with Tony Curtis. His clever, witty performances in *The Man with the Golden Gun*, *The Spy Who Loved Me*, *Moonraker*, *For Your Eyes Only*, *Octopussy* and *A View to a Kill* made him one of the most famous and popular actors in the world. In 1999 he received the CBE for his services to British film and in 2003, Roger Moore received a knighthood for his services to UNICEF for which he continues to work tirelessly.

Harold Pinter was born in London in 1930. He is married to Antonia Fraser. In 1995 he won the David Cohen British Literature Prize, awarded for a lifetime's achievement in literature. In 1996 he was given the Laurence Olivier Award for a lifetime's achievement in the-atre. In 2002 he was made a Companion of Honour for services to literature. In 2005 he received the Wilfred Owen Award for Poetry, the Franz Kafka Award (Prague) and the Nobel Prize for Literature.

Juliet Stevenson joined the Royal Shakespeare Company from RADA where she won the coveted Gold Bancroft Medal. She is an acclaimed classical actress at both the RSC and the Royal National Theatre. In 1992 her West End performance in *Death and The Maiden* won the Laurence Olivier Award for Best Actress. In film, her per-formance in *Truly, Madly, Deeply* won her the *Evening Standard* Award for Best Actress and her other film credits include *Being Julia*, *Pierrepoint* and *Breaking and Entering*. Juliet Stevenson was awarded the CBE in 1999 for her services to the British film industry and the London stage.

Harriet Walter started her career at the Royal Shakespeare Company where in 1988 her performances in *Twelfth Night* and *The Three Sisters* won the Laurence Olivier Award for Best Actress in a Revival. She was an acclaimed Cleopatra in their production of *Antony and Cleopatra*. Her stunning portrayal of Queen Elizabeth I in Schiller's *Mary Stuart* won the *Evening Standard* Award for Best Actress and a Laurence Olivier Award nomination. Film and television credits include *Sense and Sensibility*, *London* and *George Eliot*. She won the Sony Radio Award for Best Actress both in 1989 and 1991. In 2000, Harriet Walter was awarded a CBE for her services to acting in British film, theatre and television.

COPYRIGHT ACKNOWLEDGEMENTS

sion of Penguin Group (USA) Inc; all poems also from *Complete Poems* (Faber, 1984) reprinted by permission of the publishers, Faber and Faber Ltd.

Sylvia Plath: 'The Applicant', 'Death and Co', 'Lady Lazarus', 'Daddy', and 'Edge' from *Ariel*, copyright © 1961, 1962, 1963, 1965, 1966 by Ted Hughes, Foreword by Robert Lowell, reprinted by permission of HarperCollins Publishers; 'Two Views of a Cadaver Room', 'The Colossus', and 'Mushrooms' from *The Colossus and Other Poems*, copyright © 1957, 1958, 1959, 1960, 1961, 1962, reprinted with permission of Alfred A. Knopf, a division of Random House, Inc.; all poems also from *Ariel* (Faber, 1965) and *The Colossus* (Faber, 1967), all reprinted by permission of the publishers, Faber and Faber Ltd.

William Butler Yeats: 'The Pity of Love', 'The Folly of Being Comforted', 'Friends', 'Before the World was Made', 'Easter, 1916', 'Adam's Curse', 'The Municipal Gallery Revisited', and 'The Circus Animals' Desertion', all from *The Collected Poem of W B Yeats*, edited by Richard J Finneran (Macmillan, 1983), reprinted by permission of A P Watt Ltd on behalf of Michael B Yeats.

Although we have tried to trace and contact copyright holders before publication, in some cases this has not been possible. If contacted we will be pleased to rectify any errors or omissions at the earliest opportunity.

SOURCE NOTES

Introduction, pp. 1–5

p. 1 'In the beginning was the Word': John, 1: 1, *The New Oxford Bible* (Oxford University Press, 2001)

p. 1 'the holy time is quiet as a nun/breathless with adoration': William Wordsworth, *The Oxford Dictionary of Quotations* (Oxford University Press, 1979)

p. 2 'footfalls'/'in the memory': T. S. Eliot, *Four Quartets* (Faber and Faber, 1944)

p. 2 'one man loved the pilgrim soul in you': W. B. Yeats, *Selected Poetry* (Penguin Group, 1991)

p. 2 'all smiles stopped together': Robert Browning, *Poems selected by Douglas Dunn* (Faber and Faber, 1957)

p. 3 'one person talking to another': T. S. Eliot, *On Poetry and Poets* (Faber and Faber, 1957)

p. 3 'the supreme fiction': Wallace Stevens, *Collected Poetry and Prose* (Library of America, 1997)

p. 3 'If it makes my whole body': Connie Ann Kirk, *Emily Dickinson, A Biography* (Greenwood Press, 2004)

p. 3 'a way of taking Life by the throat': Elizabeth Sergeant, *Robert Frost: The Trial by Existence* (Rinehart & Winston, 1960)

p. 3 'the arrogant oligarchy': G. K. Chesterton, *Heretics* (The Bodley Head, 1905)

p. 3 'A poet always writes': R. F. Foster, *W. B. Yeats, A Life, II, The Arch-Poet* (Oxford University Press, 2003)

p. 3 'They queued and fought for tickets': Valerie Grove, *Evening Standard*, June 1987

221

p. 3 'a little different/the different way of saying it': T. S. Eliot, *On Poetry and Poets* (Faber and Faber, 1957)

p. 4 'the auditory imagination'/'the feeling for syllable and rhythm': T. S. Eliot, quoted, Seamus Heaney, *The Government of the Tongue* (Faber and Faber, 1988)

p. 4 'I have never been able to retain'/'have often a network': T. S. Eliot, ibid.

p. 4 'the sound of sense': Jay Parini, *Robert Frost: A Life* (William Heinemann, 1988)

p. 5 'Poetry helps us to speak to ourselves': Harold Bloom, *How to Read and Why* (Fourth Estate, 2001)

p. 5 'Writing with your ear to the voice',/'language, caught alive': Jay Parini, *Robert Frost: A Life* (William Heinemann, 1988)

p. 5 'what I heard made sense'/'bigness of the structure'/'opacity of thought'/'what was hypnotic': Seamus Heaney, *Finders Keepers: Selected Prose 1971–2001* (Faber and Faber, 2002)

p. 5 'clearing out of poetry every phrase': W. B. Yeats, *Selected Poems* (Penguin Group, 1991)

p. 5 'No poem, which when mastered': Edward Mendelson (ed.), *The English Auden* (Faber and Faber, 1977)

W. H. Auden, pp. 7–13

p. 9 'Truth out of Time': James Vinson (ed.), Great Writers of the English Language, Poets (Macmillan Press, 1979)

p. 9 'One Sunday afternoon in March 1922': Edward Mendelson (ed.), *The English Auden* (Faber and Faber, 1977)

p. 9 'That he turned out to be a brilliant poet': John Bayley, *The Power of Delight: A Lifetime in Literature: Essays 1962–2002* (W. W. Norton & Company, 2005)

p. 9 'Poetry . . . memorable speech': W. H. Auden, *The Poet's Tongue* (Faber and Faber, 1935)

p. 9 'the deserts of the heart': W. H. Auden, *Selected Poems* (Faber and Faber, 1979)

p. 10 'the wrong blond': Charles Osborne, *W. H. Auden: The Life of a Poet* (Eyre Methuen Ltd, 1980)

p. 10 'The triple situation': ibid.

p. 10 'If equal affection cannot be': W. H. Auden, *Selected Poems* (Faber and Faber, 1979)

p. 10 'In so far as poetry, or any of the arts': John Bayley, *The Power of Delight: A Lifetime in Literature: Essays 1962–2002* (W. W. Norton & Company, 2005)

p. 10 'I felt myself invaded by a power': Edward Mendelson (ed.), *W. H. Auden: Collected Poems* (Faber and Faber, 1976)

p. 10 'We are, I know not how, double in ourselves': Charles Osborne, *W. H. Auden: The Life of a Poet* (Eyre Methuen Ltd, 1980)

p. 11 'intellect and intuition . . . feeling and sensation': W. H. Auden, *Collected Poems* (Faber and Faber, 1976)

p. 11 'Lay your sleeping head, my love': W. H. Auden, *Collected Poems* (Faber and Faber, 1976)

p. 11 'I shall probably die alone': Charles Osborne, *W. H. Auden: The Life of a Poet* (Eyre Methuen Ltd, 1980)

p. 11 'the nicest way . . . it's cheap and it's quick': ibid.

p. 11 'the folded lie,/The romantic lie'/'We must love another or die': Edward Mendelson (ed.), *The English Auden* (Faber and Faber, 1977)

The Poems

p. 12 'When I find myself in the company': W. H. Auden, *The Dyer's Hand* (Vintage International, 1968)

p. 12 'Beauty is truth, truth beauty': John Keats, *The Complete Poems* (Penguin Books, 1973)

p. 12 'magnificently sane': Seamus Heaney, *Finders Keepers: Selected Prose 1971–2001* (Faber and Faber, 2002)

p. 12 'the inimitable Thirties fear'/'The poetry is in the blaming': Philip Larkin, *Further Requirements* (Faber and Faber, 2001)

p. 13 'For me, personally, it was a very important poem': Humphrey Carpenter, *W. H. Auden, A Biography.* (George Allen & Unwin Ltd, 1981)

p. 13 'Give me chastity . . . but not yet': St Augustine, *Confessions*, Book 8, Chapter 7

Emily Dickinson, pp. 33–40

p. 35 'Heavenly Hurt': *Emily Dickinson: The Complete Poems* (Faber and Faber, 1975)

p. 35 'pure and terrible such as I have found in no other': *Emily Dickinson, Poems selected by Ted Hughes* (Faber and Faber, 1968)

p. 36 'Charge your style with life': quoted in Thomas H. Johnson (ed.), *Emily Dickinson: The Complete Poems* (Faber and Faber, 1975)

p. 36 'The impression of a wholly new and original': ibid.

p. 36 'Strangeness . . . one of the prime requirements': Harold Bloom, *The Western Canon* (Riverhead Books, 1994)

p. 36 'as individual a thinker as Dante': ibid.

p. 36 'I smile when you suggest that I delay': *Emily Dickinson: The Complete Poems* (Faber and Faber, 1975)

p. 36 'I don't go from home': *Emily Dickinson, Poems selected by Ted Hughes* (Faber and Faber, 1968)

p. 37 '3 or 4 families': R. W. Chapman (ed.), *Jane Austen's Letters* (Oxford University Press, 1952)

p. 37 'tranced suspense': *Emily Dickinson: Poems selected by Ted Hughes* (Faber and Faber, 1968)

p. 37 'Friday I tasted life. It was a vast morsel': T. H. Johnson (ed.), *The Letters of Emily Dickinson*, vol. 2 (1958)

p. 37 'the smallest event an immensity': *Emily Dickinson: Poems selected by Ted Hughes* (Faber and Faber, 1968)

p. 37 'very wantonness of overstatement', 'his half-cracked poetess', 'I was never with anyone who drained': ibid.

p. 37 'nun of Amherst': . . . *She was commonly referred to by the villagers*

p. 37 She described herself as 'small, like the Wren . . .': *Emily Dickinson: Poems selected by Ted Hughes* (Faber and Faber, 1968)

p. 38 'vision, and the crowded, beloved creation around her and

Death – became her Holy Trinity': ibid.

p. 38 '. . . drama of erotic loss': Harold Bloom, *The Western Canon* (Riverhead Books, 1994)

p. 38 'unusual endowment of love was not going to be asked for': *Emily Dickinson: Poems selected by Ted Hughes* (Faber and Faber, 1968)

The Poems

p. 39 'One's mind had better be at its rare best': Harold Bloom, *The Western Canon* (Riverhead Books, 1994)

p. 40 'odd', 'Poetry . . . an affair of sanity . . .', 'big sane boys': Philip Larkin, *Further Requirements* (Faber and Faber, 2001)

p. 40 'the mysterious implications of its own exactness': John Bayley, *The Power of Delight: A Lifetime in Literature: Essays 1962–2002* (W. W. Norton & Company, 2005)

T. S. Eliot, pp. 49–59

p. 51 'I gotta use words when I talk to you': T. S. Eliot, *Collected Poems 1909–1962* (Faber and Faber, 1963)

p. 51 'We're not as good as Keats'/'Oh yes, we are': Peter Ackroyd, *T. S. Eliot* (Hamish Hamilton, 1984)

p. 51 'the capacity to cut into our consciousness with the sharpness of a diamond': Presentation Speech by Anders Österling, Permanent Secretary of the Swedish Academy in 1948.

p. 51 'There is a direct line which can be traced from Virgil': Ted Hughes, speech, Avron Foundation event

p. 51 'a quiet, remote figure': Peter Ackroyd, *T. S. Eliot* (Hamish Hamilton, 1984)

p. 51 'the Pope of Russell Square': ibid.

p. 51 'dull, dull, dull': ibid.

p. 52 'the boring Europeanised American': ibid.

p. 52 'Classical in literature, Royalist in politics': ibid.

p. 52 'They never did less than was expected of them': ibid.

p. 52 'how sharp and complete and sui generis': ibid.

p. 53 'I am very immature for my age, very timid, very inexperienced': Valerie Eliot (ed.), *The Letters of T. S. Eliot* (Faber and Faber, 1988)

p. 53 'The more perfect the artist, the more completely separate in him will be the man who suffers and the mind which creates': T. S. Eliot, *The Sacred Wood* (Methuen, 1920)

p. 53 'the gifts reserved for age','. . . the awareness, of things ill done': T. S. Eliot, *Four Quartets* (Faber and Faber, 1944)

p. 54 'private words addressed to you in public': T. S. Eliot, *The Complete Poems and Plays* (Faber and Faber, 1969)

p. 54 'The dead writers are that which we know': T. S. Eliot, *The Sacred Wood* (Faber and Faber, 1920)

p. 54 'Tradition is not a dead load which we drag along with us': Gustaf Hellström of the Swedish Academy, 1948

The Waste Land

p. 55 'the almost drugged and haunted condition': Peter Ackroyd, *T. S. Eliot* (Hamish Hamilton, 1984)

p. 55 'echoic quality which requires the inflection': ibid.

p. 55 'the great knockout up to date': ibid.

p. 56 'wonderful, wonderful': ibid.

p. 56 'I have done a rough draft but do not know': Valerie Eliot (ed.), *The Letters of T. S. Eliot* (Faber and Faber, 1988)

p. 56 'Tom's mind? I am Tom's mind': Peter Ackroyd, *T. S. Eliot* (Hamish Hamilton, 1984)

p. 56 'brought to her no happiness': Valerie Eliot (ed.), *The Letters of T. S. Eliot* (Faber and Faber, 1988)

p. 56 'The interior of Eliot's poetry is deeply personal': John Bayley, *The Power of Delight: A Lifetime in Literature: Essays 1962–2002* (W. W. Norton & Company, 2005)

p. 56 'My experience falls within my own circle': Eliot, note to *The Waste Land*, (Faber and Faber, 1972)

p. 56 'Have you ever been in such incessant pain': Valerie Eliot (ed.), *The Letters of T. S. Eliot* (Faber and Faber, 1988)

p. 57 'All great art is based on a condition': Peter Ackroyd, *T. S. Eliot* (Hamish Hamilton, 1984)

p. 57 'Complimenti, you bitch. I am wracked': Valerie Eliot (ed.), *The Letters of T. S. Eliot* (Faber and Faber, 1988)

'The Love Song of J. Alfred Prufrock'
'Portrait of A Lady'
'The Hollow Men'

p. 58 'It is an art of the nerves, this art of Laforgue': C. K. Stead, *The New Poetic* (Continuum, 2005)

p. 58 'Eliot followed his nerves in Prufrock': C. K. Stead, *The New Poetic* (Continuum, 2005)

p. 58 'heartlessly indifferent to its fate': Peter Ackroyd, *T. S. Eliot* (Hamish Hamilton, 1984)

p. 58 'it's completely insane': ibid.

p. 58 'a young man': C. K. Stead, *The New Poetic* (Continuum, 2005)

p. 58 'I'm afraid that J. Alfred Prufrock': ibid.

p. 59 'Between the acting of a dreadful thing/And the first motion': Shakespeare, *Julius Caesar*, II, i. 63–5

p. 59 'Rare music': Seamus Heaney, *Finders Keepers: Selected Prose 1971–2001* (Faber and Faber, 2002)

Rudyard Kipling, pp. 79–86

p. 81 'to dig with': Seamus Heaney, *Death of a Naturalist* (Faber and Faber, 1966)

p. 81 'is not only serious, he has a vocation': T. S. Eliot: *On Poetry and Poets* (Faber and Faber, 1957)

p. 81 'Kipling is the only living person not head of state': David Gilmour, *The Long Recessional: The Imperial Life of Rudyard* (John Murray, 2002)

p. 81 'In the street outside his hotel . . .': Andrew Lycett (ed.), *Rudyard Kipling, The Complete Verse* (Kyle Cathie, 2002)

p. 82 'He was further away from being a fascist than the most humane': George Orwell, *Essays* (Everyman, 2002)

p. 82 'neither evil nor anti-semitic': John Bayley, *The Power of Delight: A Lifetime in Literature, Essays 1962–2002* (W. W. Norton & Company, 2005)

p. 82 'English Literature has no adequate account': C. Carrington (ed.), *The Complete Barrack-Room Ballads* (Methuen, 1973)

p. 82 'He had far more interest in the common soldier': George Orwell, *Essays* (Everyman, 2002)

p. 82 'the flannelled fools at the wickets or the muddied oafs at the goals': Rudyard Kipling, *The Complete Verse* (Kyle Cathie, 2002)

p. 82 'The Kipling Whom Nobody Read': John Bayley, *The Power of Delight: A Lifetime in Literature, Essays 1962–2002* (W. W. Norton & Company, 2005)

p. 82 'the most complete man of genius I have ever met': David Gilmour, *The Long Recessional* (Pimlico, 2003)

p. 82 'the most inscrutable of authors': T. S. Eliot: *On Poetry and Poets* (Faber and Faber, 1957)

p. 83 'serene and tolerant man': Andrew Lycett, *Rudyard Kipling* (Weidenfeld & Nicolson, 1999)

p. 83 'all Celt and three parts fire': ibid.

p. 83 'It was impossible to predict how she would react': ibid.

p. 83 'the brute instinct for the beat': ibid.

p. 83 'House of Desolation': Rudyard Kipling, *Something of Myself* (Cambridge University Press, 1990)

p. 83 'Family Square': Andrew Lycett, *Rudyard Kipling* (Weidenfeld & Nicolson, 1999)

p. 84 'the long-haired literati': Rudyard Kipling, *The Complete Verse* (Kyle Cathie, 2002)

p. 84 'fellow craftsman's output': Rudyard Kipling, *Something of Myself* (Cambridge University Press, 1990)

p. 84 'the poet of work': ibid.

p. 84 'Writers must recognise the gulf': Andrew Lycett, *Rudyard Kipling* (Weidenfeld & Nicolson, 1999)

p. 84 'the savage wars of peace': Rudyard Kipling, *The Complete Verse* (Kyle Cathie, 2002)

p. 84 'He was capable of experience': T. S. Eliot, *On Poetry and Poets* (Faber and Faber, 1957)

p. 84 'There is always something alien about Kipling': ibid.

The Poems

p. 85 'The King's Trumpeter': John Bayley, *The Power of Delight: A Lifetime in Literature, Essays 1962–2002* (W. W. Norton & Company, 2005)

p. 85 'not only was England drained – so was Kipling': Andrew Lycett, *Rudyard Kipling* (Weidenfeld & Nicolson, 1999)

p. 86 'little ruled exercise books used to practise': ibid.

p. 86 'saw war as an obligation, but he never sang of victory': Jorge Luis Borges, *The Total Library, Non-fiction, 1922–1968* (Penguin Press, 2000)

p. 86 'Here's Literature! Here's Literature, at last': Rudyard Kipling, *The Complete Verse* (Kyle Cathie, 2002)

p. 86 'in the combination of heavy beat', 'movement of the men': T. S. Eliot, *On Poetry and Poets* (Faber and Faber, 1957)

p. 86 'A humanitarian is always a hypocrite': George Orwell, *Essays* (Everyman, 2002)

p. 86 '8,246 men out of 10,000': David Roberts (ed.), *Minds at War* (Saxon Books, 1996)

p. 86 'One can't let one's friends' and neighbours' sons': Andrew Lycett, *Rudyard Kipling* (Weidenfeld & Nicolson, 1999)

Philip Larkin, pp. 117–24

p. 119 'I like to read about people who have done nothing spectacular': Andrew Motion, *Philip Larkin, A Writer's Life* (Faber and Faber, 1993)

p. 120 'enjoy or endure': Philip Larkin, *All That Jazz, A Recorded Diary 1961–68* (The Marvell Press and Faber and Faber, 1970)

p. 120 'Hushed atmosphere': *Larkin at Sixty* (Faber and Faber, 1982)

p. 120 'What was the rock my gliding childhood struck?': Philip Larkin, *Collected Poems* (The Marvell Press and Faber and Faber, 1988)

p. 120 'A man *is* what he is paid for': ibid.

p. 120 'Poetry, that rare bird, has flown away': ibid.

p. 120 'What will survive of us is love': Philip Larkin, *Collected Poems* (The Marvell Press and Faber and Faber, 1988)

p. 120 'too clever to live': Philip Larkin, *Required Writing, Miscellaneous Pieces 1955–1982* (Faber and Faber, 1983) handwritten notes in A. L. Rowse's copy, now in author's possession

p. 120 'Kindly face, no kidding him', 'perverse psychology, Irish perhaps': ibid.

p. 121 'miss out on the big experiences of life': Andrew Motion, *Philip Larkin: A Writer's Life* (Faber and Faber, 1993)

p. 121 'deprivation', 'what daffodils were to Wordsworth': Philip Larkin, *Required Writing, Miscellaneous Pieces 1955–1982* (Faber and Faber, 1983)

p. 121 'When I think of my *twenties* or even my *thirties*': Andrew Motion, *Philip Larkin, A Writer's Life* (Faber and Faber, 1993)

p. 121 'the pram in the hall': Cyril Connolly, *Enemies of Promise* (Routledge, 1934)

p. 121 'perfection of the work rather than of the life': Philip Larkin, *Required Writing, Miscellaneous Pieces 1955–1982* (Faber and Faber, 1983)

p. 121 'Just as a romantic swell of feeling rises': *Larkin at Sixty* (Faber and Faber, 1982)

p. 121 'He still has you firmly by the hand as you cross the finishing line': ibid.

p. 121 'the stamp'/'the beating out of a piece of gold': ibid.

p. 121 'one of the means by which his country recognises itself': ibid.

p. 121 'I am going to the inevitable': Martin Amis, *Philip Larkin, Political Correctives* (essay, January 30, 1997)

p. 122 'but in a railway tunnel, half way through England', 'unfoolable mind': *Larkin at Sixty* (Faber and Faber, 1982)

The Poems

p. 123 'He is the only sophisticated poet today': John Bayley, *The Power of Delight: A Lifetime in Literature, Essays 1962–2002* (W. W.

Norton & Company, 2005)

p. 123 'making novels into poems': *Larkin at Sixty* (Faber and Faber, 1982)

p. 123 'as pervasive as garlic': Philip Larkin, *The North Ship* (Faber and Faber, 1965)

p. 123 'To escape from home is a life's work': Andrew Motion, *Philip Larkin, A Writer's Life* (Faber and Faber, 1993)

p. 123 'Never to have been born is best': John Calder, *The Philosophy of Samuel Beckett* (Calder Publications Ltd, 2002)

p. 123 'Clearly my Lake Isle of Innisfree': Philip Larkin, *Selected Letters 1940–1985* (Faber and Faber, 1992)

p. 124 'Hell is other people': Jean-Paul Sartre, *Huis Clos* (Penguin, 1944)

p. 124 'I see life more as an affair of solitude diversified by company': Philip Larkin, in *The New York Review of Books*, Volume 53, 2006

p. 124 'which measures our own nature': Philip Larkin, *Whitsun Weddings* (Faber and Faber, 1971)

p. 124 'poetry chose me': Philip Larkin, *Required Writing, Miscellaneous Pieces 1955–1982* (Faber and Faber, 1983)

Marianne Moore, pp. 145–50

p. 145 'I like country fairs, roller-coasters': Marianne Moore, 'Authors of 1951 Speaking for Themselves', *New York Herald Tribune* (1951)

p. 145 'Marianne Moore speaks to our condition as ballplayers', Marianne Moore, *Esquire*, [vol. 55] (1962)

p. 146 'Miss Moore's poetry forms part of the small body': T. S. Eliot, Preface, *Marianne Moore: Woman and Poet* (National Poetry Foundation, 1990)

p. 146 'Marianne Moore is one of the very few modern-day poets': *The Poems of Marianne Moore* (Faber and Faber, 2003)

p. 146 'If Miss Moore is laughing at us': Hilda Doolittle, *The Egoist* [vol. 111], (1916).

p. 146 'the rock crystal thing to see': Marianne Moore, *The Complete Poems of Marianne Moore* (Penguin, 1981)

p. 146 'the poet of the particular': Randall Jarrell, *Poetry and The Age* (Knopf, 1953)

p. 146 'The natural object is always the adequate symbol': Margaret Drabble (ed.), *The Oxford Companion to English Literature* (Oxford University Press, 2000)

p. 147 'for money or fame. To earn a living is needful': 'Idiosyncracy and Technique', The Ewing Lectures (University of California, 1956).

p. 147 'When a thing has been said so well': *A Marianne Moore Reader*, (Viking, New York, 1961)

p. 147 'with what unfreckled integrity it has all been done': *The Poems of Marianne Moore* (Faber and Faber, 2003)

p. 147 'My experience [at Bryn Mawr] gave me security': Bonnie Costello, *Marianne Moore: Selected Letters* (Penguin, 1998)

p. 148 'the savage's romance', 'accessibility to experience': *The Poems of Marianne Moore* (Faber and Faber, 2003)

p. 148 'Omissions are not accidents': ibid.

p. 148 'this is mortality/this is eternity': ibid.

p. 148 'I, too, dislike it: there are things that are important beyond all this fiddle': ibid.

The Poems

p. 149 'Making, Knowing, Judging': *W. H. Auden: Making, Knowing, Judging* (Clarendon Press, 1956)

p. 149 'insight of casual genius': Seamus Heaney, *Finders Keepers, Selected Prose 1971–2001* (Faber and Faber, 2002)

p. 150 'mad Ireland': *The English Auden* (Faber and Faber, 1977)

p. 150 'fanatic heart': W. B. Yeats, *Selected Poetry* (Penguin, 1991)

p. 150 'I am of Irish descent – wholly Celt': *Marianne Moore: Selected Letters* (Penguin, 1998)

Sylvia Plath, pp. 163–70

p. 165 'When my sleeping pill wears off': Sylvia Plath, *Letters Home* (Faber and Faber, 1976)

p. 165 'something intended': Seamus Heaney, *The Government of the Tongue* (Faber and Faber, 1988)

p. 165 'like a very efficient tool or weapon used': ibid.

p. 165 'will make my name': Sylvia Plath, *Letters Home* (Faber and Faber, 1976)

p. 165 'With these poems', 'something newly, wildly and subtly created': Robert Lowell, Introduction, *Ariel* (1st Perennial, 1999)

p. 166 'the blood jet is poetry,/There is no stopping it': Sylvia Plath, *Collected Poems* (Faber and Faber, 1981)

p. 166 'They exist in a prolonged, high-pitched ecstasy': Philip Larkin, *Required Writing, Miscellaneous Pieces 1955–1982* (Faber and Faber, 1983)

p. 166 'Those first nine years of my life sealed themselves off': Seamus Heaney, *The Government of the Tongue* (Faber and Faber, 1988)

p. 166 'You ask me why I spend my life writing/do I find entertainment?': Sylvia Plath, *Letters Home* (Faber and Faber, 1976)

p. 167 'I shall tell you something most miraculous': ibid.

p. 168 'composed very slowly, consulting her Thesaurus': Seamus Heaney: *Finders Keepers, Selected Prose 1971–2001* (Faber and Faber, 2002)

p. 168 'she'd rather live with her thesaurus than a bible on a desert island': Tim Kendall, *Sylvia Plath: A Critical Study* (Faber and Faber, 2001)

p. 168 'vision', 'do not. When will they come?': ibid.

p. 168 'Her physical energies having been depleted by illness': Sylvia Plath, *Letters Home* (Faber and Faber, 1976)

p. 168 'The indefatigable hoof-taps': Sylvia Plath, *Collected Poems* (Faber and Faber, 1981)

The Poems

p. 169 'the shock is sudden': Philip Larkin, *Required Writing, Miscellaneous Pieces 1955–1982* (Faber and Faber, 1983)

p. 169 'The possibility that she is simply trying', 'she has found her subject matter': ibid.

p. 169 'is an executive . . . [who] wants to be sure the applicant':

Sylvia Plath, *Collected Poems* (Faber and Faber, 1981)

p. 170 'is about the double or schizophrenic nature of death': ibid.

p. 170 'Here is a poem spoken by a girl with an Electra complex': ibid.

p. 170 'garish, sarcastic and profane': Camille Paglia, *Break Blow Burn* (Pantheon, 2005)

p. 170 'The speaker is a woman who has the great': Sylvia Plath, *Collected Poems* (Faber and Faber, 1981)

William Butler Yeats, pp. 189–95

p. 191 'If a powerful and benevolent spirit': R. F. Foster, *W. B. Yeats, A Life, I, The Apprentice Mage* (Oxford University Press, 1998)

p. 191 'modern Ireland thinks and does its business': R. F. Foster, *W. B. Yeats, A Life, II, The Arch Poet* (Oxford University Press, 2003)

p. 191 'He had a surrealist imagination': ibid.

p. 192 'the feeling for syllable and rhythm': ibid.

p. 192 'the auditory imagination': John Hayward (ed.), *T. S. Eliot, Selected Prose* (Penguin, 1953)

p. 192 'I would not be here were I not the symbol of that movement': R. F. Foster, *W. B. Yeats, A Life, II, The Arch Poet* (Oxford University Press, 2003)

p. 192 'You have disgraced yourselves, again': R. F. Foster, *W. B. Yeats, A Life, II, The Apprentice Mage* (Oxford University Press, 2003)

p 193 'allegedly reconnoitring assassination attempts': ibid.

p. 193 'flaming', 'began all the trouble of my life': R. F. Foster, *W. B. Yeats, A Life, I, The Apprentice Mage* (Oxford University Press, 1998)

p. 193 'the outward symbol of Satan in the world': ibid.

p. 193 'She lived in storm and strife/Her soul had such desire': W. B. Yeats, *The Collected Poems* (Macmillan & Company Ltd, 1965)

p. 193 'like lightning through me': R. F. Foster, *W. B. Yeats, A Life, I, The Apprentice Mage* (Oxford University Press, 1998)

p. 193 'capable of experience': T. S. Eliot, *On Poetry and Poets* (Faber and Faber, 1957)

p. 193 'Maturing as a poet . . . maturing as a whole man': ibid.

p. 193 'bare Ben Bulben's head': W. B. Yeats, *The Poems* (Everyman's Library, 1992)

p. 193 'Cast a cold eye/On life, on death,/Horseman, pass by': ibid.

The Poems

p. 194 'Women, Beware Women': Thomas Middleton, (Oxford World Classics)

p. 194 'I had no idea that any public event could so deeply move me': R. F. Foster, *W. B. Yeats, A Life II, The Arch Poet* (Oxford University Press, 2003)

p. 194 'a poem about the Ireland we have all served': R. F. Foster, *W. B. Yeats, A Life, II, The Arch Poet* (Oxford University Press, 2003)

p. 195 'the gifts reserved for age': T. S. Eliot, *Four Quartets* (Faber and Faber, 1944)

p. 195 'we achieve, if we do achieve, in little sedentary stitches': Timothy Webb (ed.), *W. B. Yeats, Selected Poetry* (Penguin Poetry Library, 1991)

p. 195 'Maybe at last being but a broken man': ibid.

INDEX OF FIRST LINES